AFRICAN-
AMERICAN
ALPHABET

AFRICAN-AMERICAN ALPHABET

A CELEBRATION OF AFRICAN-AMERICAN AND WEST INDIAN CULTURE, CUSTOM, MYTH, AND SYMBOL

GERALD HAUSMAN *and*
KELVIN RODRIQUES

ST. MARTIN'S PRESS
NEW YORK

Library of Congress Cataloging-in-Publication Data
Hausman, Gerald.
    African-American alphabet : a celebration of African-American and West Indian culture, custom, myth, and symbol / by Gerald Hausman and Kelvin Rodriques.
        p.   cm.
    Includes bibliographical references.
    ISBN 0-312-13919-5
    1. Afro-Americans—History—Dictionaries. 2. Afro-Americans—Social life and customs—Dictionaries. 3. Mythology, African—Dictionaries. 4. West Indians—History—Dictionaries. 5. West Indians—Social life and customs—Dictionaries. I. Rodriques, Kelvin. II. Title.
E184.5.H38   1996.
973'.0496073'003—dc20   95-25345
                                                    CIP

Excerpt from *Longing For Darkness: Kamante's Tales From Out Of Africa*, copyright © 1975, by Peter Hill Beard, reprinted by permission of Harcourt Brace & Company.

Excerpts from "The New Ships" and "The Making of the Drum" from *The Arrivants* by Edward Kamau Brathwaite (1973) by permission of Oxford University Press.

"In Honor of David Anderson Brooks, My Father" and "We Real Cool" by Gwendolyn Brooks, reprinted by permission of the author.

"Zion Train" by Sheldon Campbell, reprinted by permission of the author.

Excerpt from "The Ngoma and Muridzi we Ngoma of the Shona Peoples" by Seth Cohen, reprinted by permission of the author.

The text of "Home" from *Generations* by Sam Cornish copyright © 1968, 1969, 1970, 1971, by Sam Cornish, reprinted by permission of Beacon Press. Excerpt from *Grandmother's Pictures* by Sam Cornish, originally published by The Bookstore Press, 1974, reprinted by permission of the author. "From a Woman of Color To Her Sgt. Buffalo Braxton Rutlege, a Modest and Indecent Proposal" by Sam Cornish, reprinted by permission of the author.

Excerpt from *The Everglades: River of Grass* by Marjory Stoneman Douglas are reprinted by arrangement with R. Bemis Publishing, Ltd.; Marietta, GA 30007. Copyright © 1975 by Raymond A. Moody, M.D. All rights reserved.

Excerpt from *Duppy Talk: West Indian Tales of Mystery and Magic* by Gerald Hausman © 1994 reprinted by permission of Simon & Schuster Books for Young Readers. Excerpts from the audio book "Duppies, Drum Talk & Obeah Men: West Indian and Caribbean Folktales" by Gerald Hausman and Ray Griffin, reprinted by permission of Native Folktales, 2407 North Puget Sound, Tacoma, Washington 98406.

Excerpt from "The Devil and Stagolee" by Sid Hausman copyright © 1964 by the songwriter and reprinted with his permission.

Excerpt from *Our Grandmother's Drums* by Mark Hudson, copyright 1989, 1990; reprinted by permission of Grove/Atlantic Inc.

Selected excerpt from *Tell My Horse* by Zora Neale Hurston. Copyright © 1938 by Zora Neale Hurston. Copyright renewed © 1966 by Joel Hurston and John C. Hurston. Reprinted by permission of HarperCollins Publishers, Inc.

Excerpt from *On The Road* by Jack Kerouac. Copyright © 1955, 1957 by Jack Kerouac; renewed © 1983 by Stella Kerouac, renewed © 1985 by Stella Kerouac and Jan Kerouac. Used by permission of Viking Penguin, a division of Penguin Books USA Inc.

Excerpts from "Walk About My World" copyright © 1994 by Ross LewAllen, reprinted by permssion of the author.

Excerpts from "Forgotten Pioneers" by Scott Minerbrook, reprinted by permission of *U.S. News & World Report*.

Excerpt from *Mama Day*. Copyright © 1988 by Gloria Naylor. Reprinted by permission of Ticknor & Fields/Houghton Mifflin Company. All rights reserved.

Excerpt from *The Children of Sisyphus* by Orlando Patterson. Permission granted by Longman Group Limited.

"Bliss," "Faith," "Ladder of Love" by Kelvin Rodriques, reprinted by permission of the author.

"Home" by Rohan Savariau, reprinted by permission of the author.

Excerpts from *The Magic Island* by William Seabrook. Copyright © 1929 by W. B. Seabrook. Reprinted by permission of the author and The Watkins/Loomis Agency.

"Indigo," "Gone Home Free," and "Quilt" by Terri Lynne Singleton, reprinted by permission of the author.

"The Glory Trumpeter" from *Collected Poems 1948-1984* by Derek Walcott. Copyright © 1986 by Derek Walcott. Reprinted by permission of Farrar, Straus & Giroux, Inc.

Poem by Burning Spear by permission of Winston Rodney.

Excerpt from *Deep Like the Rivers: Stories of my Negro Friends* by Martha Emmons, a publication of the Texas Folklore Society, Nacogdoches, Texas.

"Men" by E. Ethelbert Miller from *First Light: Selected and New Poems*, Black Classic Press, 1994, by permission of the author.

Design by Janet Tingey

First Edition: February 1996

10 9 8 7 6 5 4 3 2 1

TABLE OF CONTENTS

ACKNOWLEDGMENTS

The authors wish to thank the following editors, librarians, archivists and researchers, whose contribution to the book was essential:

Senior editor, Bob Weil; associate editor, Rebecca Koh; editorial assistant, Andrew Graybill, St. Martin's Press, New York, NY.

Researcher and poet, Terri Lynne Singleton, Columbus, Ohio; the Columbus Metropolitan Library and the Parsons Branch Library Staff, Columbus, Ohio.

Assistant archivist, Mary Giles, the Charleston Museum, Charleston, South Carolina; Christina Wieland, United Church Board for Homeland Ministries, Cleveland, Ohio.

Researcher and editor, Mariah Fox, the University of Miami Library; Professor Marceline Wittmer, Department of Art History, University of Miami.

The Library of the Institute of Jamaica, Kingston, Jamaica.

Researcher and archivist Ross LewAllen, LewAllen and LewAllen, Santa Fe, New Mexico.

Editor and typist, Laura Ware, Santa Fe, New Mexico.

In many ways the following people not only made this book possible, they made this book. Therefore, more than thanks are due. We herewith offer a silent prayer and their names: Katherine King, Washington, D.C., archive research; Mariah Fox, Miami, Florida, pen and ink illustration; Jack Lew, Kansas City Art Institute, Kansas City, Missouri, ethnic art coordination; Barbara Baumann, Santa Fe, New Mexico, African photography; Bobbe

Besold, Santa Fe, New Mexico, photography; Lisa Remeny, Tropic Arts, Coconut Grove, Florida, watercolor illustration; Ross LewAllen, Santa Fe, New Mexico, photography and illustration; R. D. Johnson, photography, St. James City, Florida; The American Center for Haitian Art, Matlacha, Florida; The Library of Congress, Prints and Photo Archive Division, Washington, D. C.; Susan Lucke, The Lowe Art Museum, the University of Miami, Miami, Florida; Marcia Parris, Publicity, HarperCollins, New York City.

INTRODUCTION
WHERE THE LEOPARDS SING LIKE BIRDS

We were speaking about Native American myths on a live radio program in San Diego when a caller, who said that he was half Native American and half African-American, asked us, "Why don't you talk about the common ground that we share, the myths that are Indian and black?" He went on to say that most African-Americans were aware of this subtle relationship—from the merging of the Seminoles with runaway slaves to the sharing of Rastafari on the Indian reservations of today. "I am serious," the caller repeated, "there are many of us who know and love these things that are red and black. You should really consider doing a book about this." What grew out of his urging is *The African-American Alphabet,* a book that explores the unique and shared heritage of African-American, West Indian, and Amerindian cultures.

We have sought in these pages to express the great wisdom of Mother Africa and to embrace that which connects all of us to the same mother and father. As poet and songwriter Ziggy Marley commented when asked if his music appealed primarily to white audiences: "Music is like water. We all need water to drink." So, like the vaudou god Damballah, the spirituality of man's birthplace, Africa, is a snake that swallows its own tail, a circle that has no beginning or end. It is inclusive, the African cosmos, without

The Preacher: Class in Session. From the Collections of the Library of Congress.

limits or boundaries of any measurable kind. Mythologically speaking, Africa covers the coverable world and as the sacred Navajo song of creation, The Beautyway, tells us, "This blessing covers all."

African mythology contains a veritable Bible of instruction on how to live, but, most importantly, it explains how to live in a sea of constant change. This is the beauty of African-American spirituality, the absence of nihilism, the presence of positive energy. The ghost that speaks from the bush and from the gilded picture frame is an ancestor, alive and well, all these long years, all these sad centuries. Out of the painful past and the uncertain future, there is always a guide, a wise counselor, a mathematician of esthetics, a bard of ancient politics, a vagabond of tricky roads and rivers, a sage who knows the snout of a crocodile from the knob of a floating stick.

From ancestors, then, come sayings. From the unforgotten people of the past come plangent thoughts, untrammeled by time. In these, we hear the arcane lore of the bush doctor, the mystic shepherd, the sign reader, the vision seer, the tale teller. In the great bush of ghosts (like the universal library sought, in trance, by psychic Edgar Cayce) there awaits the chanting shaman, the dreaming pharaoh, and the historic surgeon.

And the road to all of these lost ancestors is simply the African-American family.

We sought storytellers in three major geographical areas: West Africa, the West Indies, and the North American South. When people ask, and they often do, how we find such stories, the response that comes to mind is "family." In the remembrance of living people, one can find the formulas and fantasies, the dreams and fables, the oral histories of the collective unconscious. From families we discover myths, from which we realize truths that open not only the crusted locks of the past but the frozen vaults of the future.

What do African-American families remember?

What do they put away, as if for all time?

They put away poems, gestures of hands, the wisdom of the heart, the color indigo, the elephant's sad eminence, the lion's loyalty, the endless brotherhood and sisterhood of rivers that flow together, the signs of life and death as foretold by clouds, rain, and cigar ashes, a tree that spirals heavenward and where the leopards sing like birds, the song of Nine Night, the permanence of the word when balanced upon the tongue, the whisperings of the universal trickster, call him Devil, Time, Legba. These are the mysteries that African-American people talk about. And they are the same things that Native Americans speak of when they gather to share their old stories.

It would be impossible, however, to introduce this book without placing it in the context of measurable history. For a great many of the symbols of African-American culture arose from slavery, and it is in the West Indies and the coastal South of the United States that they came to represent the recollection of the homeland. The occasionally subtropical, and often tropical, landscape containing swamp, seacoast, savannah, and jungle, brought back immediate memories of Africa, and ready remedies of escape. These were psychic journeys as well as physical ones and through them one could dream, remember, and, most important, heal. Moreover, using a vast materia medica and folklorica the enslaved could, and did, freely transform their world from one of subjection to one of possession. Thus they turned captivity into activity, capture into covenance, as in the case of West Indian Maroons, who negotiated and won their freedom.

Between the seventeenth and nineteenth centuries, slavery— the importation of black people from West Africa, let us say, to the Caribbean and America—involved the longest and largest and most depraved system of manpower in human de-evolutionary history. Over a period of perhaps four hundred years, some six hundred million African people were forcibly removed from their homeland. One of the results of this dehumanization, though, was not negative, but positive. For this deplorable system of slavery gave rise to an incongruous form of bargaining power: mysticism. While slavery tortured all who came under its rule, it nonetheless gave birth to supernatural forces. The ceremonials of spiritual greatness came back from African memory, and the old African gods emerged from the veils of smoke and dream.

However, the relationship between master and subject has been well covered in other volumes. The focus of this one is to show the means by which displaced Africans sought empowerment through the disciplines of magic, dance, drum, song, and, especially, myth. These ritual forms of mythical recitation sustained them and gave future generations a new life from the dying order of an older one.

What are the ritual myths spoken of here?

They are the practices of folkloric beings—heroes and real people—who presented themselves on the historical scene, making life a little more bearable for those who knew or had heard of them. Such a near deity was John Henry, the steel-driving man, the one who laid down America's railroad tracks, in sunlight and starlight. He was, by all reports, nothing less than a black David pitted against an industrial-age Goliath, the power-driven steam drill. And this legendary man, who had a real existence in America, was nothing less than one of the many avatars of High John the Conqueror, the African-imported superman.

The messengers of the gods were many and they came in many forms, sometimes demigod, sometimes common man. We hear of Anansi, the spider god, originally a trickster overcome by a king who smashed him into pieces, little shadows that turned into spiders. And these, they say, inspired men to magical deeds; among those inspired was one of the characters in this book, Uncle Time, a real-life shaman living today in the West Indies. Legba, the African Keeper of the Gate, an intercessor with the gods, has multiple identities, as has Damballah, the snake deity. In every case, the legend inspired a mortal to reach out to destiny and to change the world that we live in.

Thus, such historical and mystical leaders as Toussaint Louverture of Haiti and Marie Laveau of New Orleans drew sustenance from the roots culture of Africa, producing a spiritual brew of nouveau vaudou to intoxicate their followers.

Witchcraft, magic, and medicine frequently cross lines from good to bad and back again. In African lore, good is not an absolute, nor is evil a discrete demon, or entity. Both are qualities that can exchange identities. The Devil, as presented by white Baptists of European descent, was depicted as evil. However, he got a surprising response from African slaves, who found him both tolerable and believable, as well as entertaining. After all, Old Scratch evinced power; like all deities, he might be persuaded to use it recklessly, but, on the other hand, he might, if willing, give an oppressed person some needed help. He did so, of course, in the myth of Stagolee, the famed black bad man who haunted the Southeast and West.

So this is a book of African-American and West Indian mythology that sheds light on how men and women turned to the old ways to nurture themselves. It shows how they turned to the wisdom of warriors, elders, poets, priests, storytellers, and yarn spinners to continue a journey that did not end, but just began, in what was mistakenly called the New World. The emphasis here is not religious in the strictest sense; rather, we want to show the art of day-to-day life through myth. We see in these pages the self-contained magic of individuals, alive today and remembered in the past, who strengthened the survival of a people far from home.

Overall the book shows how valuable archetypes—merely by being honored—can lift the hearts of those who must bear the hardest burden of all: humdrum, day's done, wake-up-in-the-morning-and-go-to-work life. In the chapter on quilts, black poet Terri Lynne Singleton quotes an African-American quilter: "These old hands made that." But it is not the hands that speak, it is the fabric scraps themselves. They tell, heroically, of "hard lives and soft babies" that were once cradled beneath the gentle visions and sweet revelations of African elders, people who had to leave behind something of themselves in order to keep the spirit of Africa alive. These voices, musically woven together in *The African-American Alphabet,* speak wonderfully of positive values. "Here I am," they whisper. "I'm talking to you." We can learn from them today; for, as it is said, "No past, no future." Let us join hands. And listen.

GERALD HAUSMAN and KELVIN RODRIQUES

AFRICAN-
AMERICAN
ALPHABET

AMISTAD

On June 26, 1839, the *Amistad* left Havana carrying fifty-three Africans and their Spanish captors towards two very different futures: slavery and profit. However, three days out of port, the Mendi leader, whose name was Sengbe and who was known as Cinque to the Spanish, led an uprising against Captain Ramon Ferrer. As a result, Ferrer was killed, the Africans were freed, and Sengbe took command of the *Amistad*.

Sengbe's intention was to steer the ship east to Africa; however, the two remaining Spaniards tricked him, sailing east by day, and by night sailing west with the stars. For two months, the Amistad went upon its meandering course, heading ever closer to the American mainland. On August 26, 1839, the U.S. Coast Guard ship *Washington* encountered the *Amistad*. Shortly thereafter, Sengbe was arrested and the slave ship was towed to New London, Connecticut. Once the story of the Spanish crew was told, the African slaves, prisoners at the outset of their voyage, became chained again.

The story of the *Amistad* is debated. Laced with conflicting legality—the ship belonging to Spain, the cargo belonging to Africa and Spain—the courtroom arguments went back and forth. Spain asked for ship and cargo to be returned. But Sengbe and his Mendi companions argued forcefully that they had been kidnapped, and that kidnapping was illegal. The case became an instant *cause célèbre*, involving such influential leaders as Roger Baldwin, the principal defense attorney, and William Lloyd Garri-

Sengbe, the Liberator. Drawing by Mariah Fox.

Amistad Mendians. Drawing by Devon Himes, Kansas City Art Institute.

son, editor of the antislavery paper *The Liberator*. One week after the ship's capture, a group known as the Amistad Committee was formed; its goal was to set the Africans free.

One of the many difficulties encountered in the succeeding court case, which rose all the way to the Supreme Court, was the issue of translation. How could these imprisoned members of the Mendi tribe speak clearly in their own defense when no one understood their own complex language? A search of the New York dockyards led to the discovery of a native Mendi named James Corey, whose efforts at explicating the plight of his people were successful.

Now the Amistad Committee finally enlisted the aid of former President John Quincy Adams. Although he had not argued a case before the high court in over thirty years, his keen arguments were heard, and the court, after much deliberation, found itself in favor of freeing the stolen Africans.

The Amistad Committee then raised funds and sent the thirty-five Mendi survivors back to their homeland. By then, many of them had learned some English, and one member of their group, a man named Kinna, was able to write a letter, which was received by his benefactor: "We have been on great water. Not any danger fell upon us. . . . if I never see you in this world, we will meet in heaven."

So it was that a ship destined to carry human cargo as slaves was emptied of its purpose. And so it was also that men captured

Above: Mutiny of Amistad. Engraving, from the Collections of the Library of Congress.
Background: Mutiny Motif. Drawing by Teri Sanders, Kansas City Art Institute.

and tried for mutiny and piracy were found innocent of all charges; and the very society that charged them looked into the mirror of its undoing, and recognized that the judgment it had made was turned upon itself. More than twenty-five years prior to the abolition of slavery in America, this court battle determined that the human spirit could not be thus abused. Cinque, the son of an African king, the man named Sengbe, went back to Africa with his crew of free men, knowing that though many thousands of his brothers and sisters had gone into chains, the auction block was not for him and his shipmates.

ANCESTOR

MEN
my father and brother
have no wings
their legs are short
and cannot reach the ground

when i left home
i left walking on my head
i decided i would give birth
to a leopard

i stopped at the place
where the river disappears
into the sky

those of us who are birds
envy the leopard
even the strange ones
who call themselves men
hide inside their shells
— E. ETHELBERT MILLER

African, Djenni-Mopti (male) seat-
ed male figure; 11th–13th century
earthenware. Museum Purchase,
1991.

"Who remembers old Marcus Garvey?" asks the political-mystical
poet Burning Spear. Who, indeed? Marcus Garvey and his Black
Star Line and the mythical ship of redemption that was designed
to return African Americans to Africa. Here was the ancestor ship
of dream and legend, an *Amistad* for everyone, returning the
grandchildren to the Gold Coast whence they sprang, whence

they were taken in chains through the watery hells of the Middle Passage. An old Jamaican friend of mine told me that after Marcus Garvey, the great African-Jamaican liberationist, was thrown in jail for U.S. mail fraud—a trumped-up charge—the stock certificates of his black-owned and black-operated shipping line were used to wallpaper the tuck-shop shanties of the West Indian hills. Garvey's dream, abstract as it may seem to some, was to deliver his people, like Moses, back to the place of their birth. How different was this from the dreams of actual slaves, who as they lay dying, believed their souls would return in phantom flight across the seas to their home?

> . . . *Mammies crowded with cloths,*
> *flowered and laughed;*
> *white teeth*
> *smooth voices like pebbles*
> *moved by the sea of their language,*
>
> *Akwaaba they smiled*
> *meaning welcome*
>
> *Akwaaba they called*
> *aye kood*
>
> *Well have you walked*
> *have you journeyed*
>
> *welcome.*
>
> *You who have come*
> *back a stranger*
> *after three hundred years*
>
> *welcome.*
> — FROM "THE NEW SHIPS," BY EDWARD BRATHWAITE

The ancestor tree or cotton tree of the West Indies (and similar broad-trunked, majestic trees of the southern United States) has long been associated with spirits. The Arawak people made dugout canoes of the tree and invested it with legends; so did the Maya of Guatemala, and the Ashanti of Africa, who called it the god tree. In Jamaica, it is also known by this name, and is widely regarded with ancestral awe. This nearly universal African belief in the spiritual power conferred upon humankind by trees in whose roots ancestors dwell is exemplified by the Batanga belief in the birth-tree and its identity with the child for whom it is planted. In Calabar, Nigeria, a young palm tree is planted when a child is born, and the afterbirth is buried under it. The afterbirth ensures the growth of the tree, as the growth of the tree ensures the growth of the child. The Hupa Indians of California, who split in two a young fir tree at the birth of a child, put the afterbirth and umbilical cord inside and bind the tree together again. The welfare of the child depends thereafter on the fate of the tree.

"One would never," Jamaican author Olive Senior writes, "put an axe to a cotton tree without first propitiating the spirits that dwell therein—most often with a sprinkling of white rum." Duppies, or ghosts, dwell at the roots of the tree and exfoliate through limb, branch, and leaf. The cotton tree may live for hundreds of years, which contributes not only to its size, but also to its legendary nature. In Senegal, poet Ross LewAllen encountered the cotton tree's giant cousin, the baobab:

I see the grandfather tree, the baobab
ball of sun balancing on a thick branch.
The big, old, many-armed grandfather tree
is playing volleyball with the sun.

In African myth an ancestor is akin to a god and is the bearer of human burdens, yet somehow answerable to no one. The Ibo, for example, were governed not by kings and chiefs, but by gods and

ancestors, the two having joined supernatural forces, according to historians Anthony Atmore and Gillian Stacey: "The god Chukwa had created the visible universe, many of whose aspects—including the sun, the sky and the earth—existed on two levels, as matter and as spirits, or *alusi*." These ancestral spirits could bring blessing or destruction, depending upon propitiation and circumstance. Lineage and elected priests were therefore summoned to contend with these mystical and mercurial forces. Those peo-

Children of Eatonville, Florida. Photograph by Zora Neale Hurston, from the Collections of the Library of Congress.

ple who lived good lives and were properly buried according to custom would become ancestor spirits. Their world, that of the dead, was a clear reflection of the Ibo's own. They looked after the living, were frequently reborn among them, and were called the returners.

The Creator of the Bushongo, a people who probably originated near Lake Chad, was a gigantic being named Bumba. They say that in the beginning he existed alone in a universe consisting entirely of water. One day, feeling internal pains, Bumba vomited up the sun, moon, and stars, thus giving light to the world. He then coughed up the leopard, the crested eagle, and the crocodile. And all these were the ancient parents of creatures that exist today. Bumba, the Creator, was known to the Bushongo by the name of First Ancestor.

There is an old Ashanti saying: "When you follow in the path of your father, you learn to walk like him." Kenyan storyteller Richard Tito Ama, speaking of the customs of western Kenya, stated: "We believe that when a person is gone physically, he is still with us spiritually. When a grandfather is about to die, he says: 'Okay, my people, I am dying. But don't think while I'm gone, that I'm gone for good. For I am still with you and I will be seeing whatever is happening in this home. So I want you to live in peace and live together as I have been living with you.'"

However, for the living, those other returners—expatriates repatriating, dreamers dreaming—the ancestor path is not without claws and thorns, delusions and dangers:

I tossed my net
but the net caught
no fish

I dipped a wish
but the well
was dry

Beware
beware
beware

I travelled to a distant town
I could not find my mother
I could not find my father
I could not hear the drum
Whose ancestor am I?
— FROM "THE NEW SHIPS," BY EDWARD BRATHWAITE

The answer lies not in repatriation, for Africa is yet afire, crackling under to the tensions of decades of colonial and postcolonial rule. In the late fifties, when Garvey's dream was actually realized, Jamaican families journeyed to Ethiopia and lived on farmland donated by Emperor Haile Selassie. After some years, the disappointing results of communal farming bogged down in the familiar echo: Whose ancestor am I? In the end, the families were returned to Jamaica and the Emperor dissolved the commission he had created to study resettlement for Caribbean people in Ethiopia.

If it seems impossible to go forward, or back, on the long sinuous ancestor path, what choice is there? In conflagration lies suffering, and the revenge wreaked upon the past by the present leaves only a bleak flash of the future. Here is the wisdom of the classic lyric composed by the sixties reggae group the Heptones:

Isn't it strange
How princesses and kings
In clown-ragged capers
In sawdust rings
While common people
Like you and me
Will be the builders
For eternity
Each is given

A bag of tools
A shapeless mask
And a Book of Rules
   (COPYRIGHT © ACKEE MUSIC, INC.)

It is the common thread, then, the fabric of family, sewn tightly together in the worst of times, that is the people's saving grace. In the words of one African-American family who went to Africa in the sixties: "We learned to care about people who were really different from us. We learned self-assurance, a greater sense of being black . . . feet-on-the-ground-strength. . . . We have taught our own children to be responsible. That you can be whatever you want to be, if you give it your all. We have taught our children respect without having to say, Yes, sir, or Yes, ma'am."

In answer to the echo of fear—Whose ancestor am I?—Ziggy Marley says, "*Earth is my mother, there is no other.*"

BANJO

On American plantations, African exiles did not beat drums and chant songs that harked back to Africa, nor were they encouraged to do so by the plantation owners. One might imagine that, given time and acclimatization, they would gravitate toward a plucked instrument like the guitar, an instrument much less forbidding than the ominous-toned skin drum, but in fact, this did not happen until much later during the post-slavery era.

However, West African blacks, brought to America in slave ships, did have an instrument common to their culture: the banjo. Made of skin and string, groundhog and cat, it was similar to instruments made by the Moors, north of the Sahara. An early French visitor to this country described it as the African *rabouquin*: "a triangular piece of board with three strings made of intestines, supported by a bridge, which may be stretched at pleasure by means of pegs like those of our instruments in Europe; it is indeed nothing else than a guitar with three strings." In 1785, Thomas Jefferson aptly remarked in a footnote of his *Notes on the State of Virginia* that the slave instrument of choice "is the Bonjar, which they brought hither from Africa . . ." A skin-covered gourd with strings, this earliest form of what we now call the banjo might also have been made from a hollowed-out turtleshell or a wooden bowl; its obvious allure was its similarity to the drum.

In the minstrelsy era of the late 1700s and early 1800s, the banjo found a beloved place. Banjoists were close in popularity to bones and tambo players, who in England were called corner

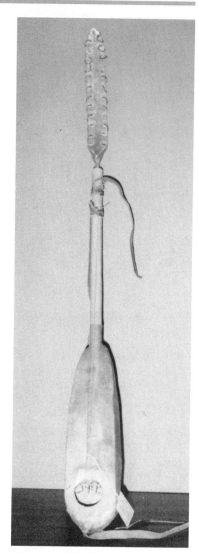

Two-string Plucked Instrument. Zaire, Africa. The Lowe Art Museum, University of Miami.

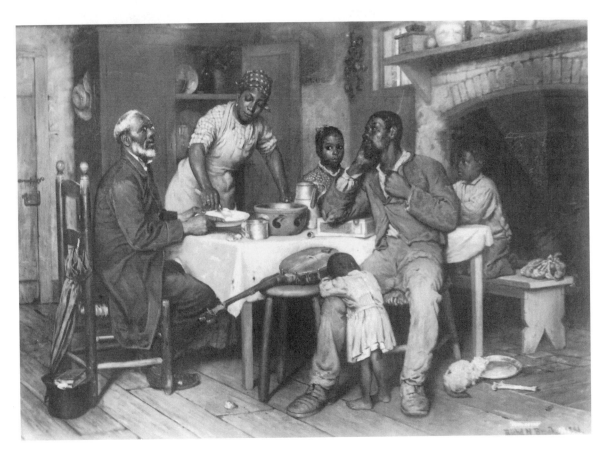

Black Family at Dinner. From the Collections of the Library of Congress.

men. Visualize, if you will, sixty performers on a stage, line upon line, rising in tiers. On the wings were the end-men with their tambourines and bones. Following their lead, in the second section of a typical minstrel show, came a rousing number of banjo-playing and clog-dancing performers whose antics fitted their musical skills. Both end-men and banjo boys had one great thing in common: The strum was the drum. And though it didn't incite rebellion, it did fly like fire and make a kind of musical contagion that was happy and sad at the same time. Part farce, part tragedy, the banjo took on a soul of its own, a ringing of rhythm that, behind a thin disguise, was none other than the forbidden Congo drum. Sand dances and clog dances were performed in glittery and airy style by apparitions in shiny suits of bright mail; and with their high-minded antics went the banjo and the bones, the fiddle, and the tambourine. For a long while, the role of the stately interlocutor, who sat in the center of the line of minstrel men, was the banjoist's. Over and over, he hammered out the rhythm beaten down and played up by his musical end-men brothers, Brother Bones and Brother Tambo. Of the four instruments cited here as the ones frequently used, the banjo would seem to be the most African, and in that respect the most "rootical." We can, furthermore, trace the Elizabethan origin of bones, the Basque source of the tambourine, and the wholly un-Ethiopian genesis of the violin. The banjo, though, strikes a pure, three-to-five-stringed note of African intensity: "Cindy got religion, she's had it once before, but when she hears my old banjo, she's the first one on the floor." It may not have been noticed by Southern gentry as an "instrument of origin," a kind of rinky-dink, rappety-tap drum with strings. On the other hand, the West African *bania*, the banjo proper, would become indispensable in American mainstream folk music. As musicologist Frederic V. Grunfeld has pointed out: "In America, where musical integration is a continuous process going back to Colonial times, the banjo player from Africa meets the guitar player from Europe, and the result is that instruments as well as styles are exchanged."

The imitative tradition, of which the banjo is student as well as teacher, is responsible for making the minstrel sound a combination of imitation Africa and authentic Europe. Gottlieb Grampner, a German oboist and bass player of the 1790s, is considered the author of the first minstrel composition. It was in Charleston that he chanced to hear a banjo being played by a black musician. Intrigued, Grampner acquired one and, to the surprise and delight of his musical counterpart, learned to play it. The rest is history. Ringing and raucous, ticklish and tricky, on came the banjo, and a new sound was born. Grampner's first banjo composition appeared in the Federal Street Theater play *Oroonoko* in Boston in 1799.

The Southern writer George Washington Cable commented:

"The grand instrument at last, the first violin, as one might say, was the banjo...for the true African dance, a dance not so much of legs and feet as of the upper half of the body, a sensual, devilish thing tolerated only by Latin-American masters, there was wanted the dark inspiration of African drums and the banjo's thump and strum." There is also the Creole song, which Mr. Cable once overheard sung by a slave. With his banjo as confidant, the singer sang of a passing dandy:

Voyez ce mulet-la, Musieau Bainjo,
Comme il est insolent;
Chapeau sur cote, Musieau Bainjo,
La canne a la main, Musieau Bainjo,
Botte quie fait crin, crin, Musieau Bainjo.

(*"Look at that mulatto there, Mr. Banjo,*
Doesn't he put on airs?
Hat cocked to the side, Mr. Banjo,
Cane in hand, Mr. Banjo
Boots that go crank, crank, Mr. Banjo.")
—TRADITIONAL CREOLE SONG

Prior to the appearance of the blues, the banjo filled in for the guitar as a kind of talkative dummy perched upon the ventriloquist's lap. It cried, it sighed, it sang like a river and rang like a stream, a volley of bells on the blue-black Southern plantation night. "From time to time," wrote the European composer Henri Iterz in the 1840s, "while listening to negro banjo players, I have pondered the mysterious law of rhythm which seems to be a universal law, since rhythm is a coordinated movement, and movement is life, and life fills the universe." So it was that four-string cheese-box banjos came into being, to float in sweet accord with the pulsations of the cosmos. The Hungarian composer Antonin Dvořák, when he was in America in the 1890s, said that "music in this country must be founded on what are called the Negro melodies." Yes, the tambourine and bones, the thigh-clap and spoons, the stomp-attack rhythm of the hard-heeled clog, the bugle-fiddle-triangle ring of that most universal of musical instruments, the banjo, who, like the stalwart old mule, carries all of these, from time immemorial, on his back.

BUFFALO SOLDIER

FROM A WOMAN OF COLOR TO HER SGT. BUFFALO BRAXTON RUTLEGE
A MODEST AND INDECENT PROPOSAL

My Buffalo soldier boy a
love song (this is)
for a man
who loves
green spring onions
from the woman
who would love
him (breath & all)
my man straight and tall
who never thought he
would see the Rio Grande
a free Negro and man
come be my lover soldier boy
where Uncle Remus serves tea
in Washington proud
of his vittles Negro white men
think black man and pure
of heart but slow in mind
come my lover straight
and tall man of the cavalry
soldier boy
man of my dreams mouth
full of fresh spring onions
— SAM CORNISH

Ashanti Horse and Rider.
The Lowe Art Museum,
University of Miami.

A flag blows in the wind before one of the sixty-one graves of Buffalo Soldiers that are scattered among the other headstones in the Philadelphia National Cemetery. "It is important to keep alive the memory of these brave individuals who gave so freely in the defense of our nation," commented cemetery director Dee Blake in a recent interview. One wonders why it has taken so long to honor, not the dead, but the living. For one of the last Buffalo Soldiers of America, Sgt. Major William Harrington III, died, within a few months of attaining the age of one hundred, in 1994.

Who were the Buffalo Soldiers and what was their contribution to the American frontier? Although African Americans fought in

Band of the 107th U.S. Colored Infantry. From the Collections of the Library of Congress.

the American Revolution and the Civil War, they were not permitted to make the military a career until 1866, when Congress created the 9th and 10th cavalries and the all-black infantry units that formed the 24th and 25th regiments.

The name and fame of "buffalo soldiers" stemmed from the Indian Wars of the late nineteenth century; the first was against the Cheyenne, along the Kansas–Pacific Railroad lines. Cheyenne warriors respected the ferocity with which the African-American men fought, and seeing their hair, dark skin, and dusty coats, they conferred upon them—even as foes—the highest honor imaginable, a name worthy of their valor. Buffalo was sage and sustenance to the Plains people, counselor and courier to the gods, keeper of summer in the bones of winter. The Buffalo Soldier, so named, was given the title as a badge of honor.

Along with fighting, stringing telegraph lines, and mapping the wilderness, the Buffalo Soldier units also controlled mobs, captured outlaws, and built and renovated army posts. They received a total of twenty-four Medals of Honor, thirteen of these earned during the Western campaigns, and many subsequent unit citations. But little of their contribution, until recently, has been known on a large scale.

Reggae prophet Bob Marley cast the Buffalo Soldier as a mystic warrior, comparing him to a dreadlock Rasta, a rebel-seer, a stranger in a strange land: "Stole him from Africa, brought him to America . . . fighting on arrival, fighting for survival." In the now-famous song, he celebrates the Buffalo Soldier's unity with Caribbean blacks, merging America and Jamaica, symbolically and spiritually. General Colin Powell, acknowledging his own affinity with the Buffalo Soldier, declared himself a "spiritual descendant" of the cavalrymen.

One imagines those first units of the 10th, out in the great grasslands and badlands, moving across the remains of an open ocean bottom from the Pliocene, among myriad shells and petrifactions, among the bleached bones of the buffalo, the mastodon, and the pterodactyl. Surrounded by the immensity of the illimitable sky comes the "African herbsman," descendant of kings, poets, scholars, alchemists, metallurgists, and scribes—the Buffalo Soldier.

The land is alive and the Buffalo Soldier sees, instinctively, that his quarry—Cheyenne, Arapaho, Kiowa, Crow—knows the living moment is also an eternal one. Hence, one may die and yet live with honor. The bond, then, between hunter and hunted is cast in unity. Between the renegade Indian and the outcast black there is brotherhood.

Today, the unity is still evident. The reggae movement is embraced by Pueblo and other Indian people of the Southwest, especially the young. Jim Beckwourth, a half-breed precursor of the Buffalo Soldier, emerged as a chief of the Absaroka, an African American–Native American, a red black man. It is as the shaman said: "A warrior creates his own identity, no matter where he is or what he does." This was the case with the Buffalo Soldier, a man apart, a man who was a part of the vastness of so many continents.

CHURCH

In the Church of the Fabled Burden,
there is no redemption
except in the wood doves
that compose the choir.

In the Church of the Confiscated Integrity,
the wood rats tap-dance upon broken
mirrors and the palmettoes pray
silently in the rafters.

In the Church of the Eternal Vehemence,
the bells toll for the Sirens of Neptune
cowrie shells shine in the cane
baskets of collection; the sun is host
to copulating chameleons.

In the Church of the Burnished Semen,
a rock shaped like a hawk's head
drips blood from its beak
upon the sacristy, but attend:
all is well,
all is well.

— FROM "NIGHT IN THE WEST INDIES," BY GERALD HAUSMAN

Preacher. Drawing by Teri Sanders,
Kansas City Art Institute.

In *The Children of Sisyphus*, by Orlando Patterson, a little church
in a valley comes down around the shoulders of the swaying
intoxicants, the parishioners dreaming of Zion. They fall, full

sway, to the magical words of incantation; and the words are a river, a torrent of exultation:

The river came down. Came gushing down. Down the veins of their flesh that swelled with heat. It was such an agony. Such a sweet, gurgling, rushing agony. It twisted the flesh that wrapped their necks. It wrenched their shoulders. Every muscle writhed. Torment. The river knows no bank. Everything goes down before it. Trees, houses, cows and rich man's castles, donkeys and American motor-cars. It was Gabriel, mighty, rhapsodic Gabriel. She held on to her sister. For joy, for pain. But Gabriel would not let go and she fell to the ground in ecstasy. And now Shadrach. Meshach. Abednego. They flung them to the ground. They burned them in the mighty furnace of their power. They ravished them and twisted them in the dust. Burn and burn and burn again. Eat up the dirt with outstretched limbs. Dying, fluttering birds. Crawl under Michael. Calm, sweet, tormenting Michael. Run from Rutibel. Oh merciful, almighty God. Run. Black cloak spreading like wings of bat. Run, Shepherd John! Do, Shepherd John. Use your staff! Can't speak. Use your staff. Useless. Dust.

They screamed in the voice of the unknown tongues. Those that were too possessed were calmed down by the Mothers and armorbearers and Shepherd John. Those that were slow were held and whirled and lashed with the staff. They leaped with anguish. They rolled and moaned in a blissful, divine paroxysms. Oh, what a writhing joy. What pain relieving pain. Oh, sweet, sweet, excruciating release.

The release and the relief that came to African Americans in church did not come accidentally to the "New World." It came as part and parcel of the river gods, the ancestor worship, the social function of festive gathering—all the mystery and mysticism of the Old World, Africa. In Catholic areas of America, for instance, Legba, the African Keeper of the Gate, got a new name and incar-

Background: The Ministerial Powers of Daddy Grace. From the Collections of the Library of Congress.

nation. In Louisiana he went from Legba to Lebba to Liba, and shared his identity with St. Peter, the Keeper of the Keys.

Since the Protestants had no saints with whom they could identify, the transplanted Africans found another personage, one whose manner was clearly reminiscent of their own trickster-messenger deities. This was none other than the Devil, and while Protestantism said that the Devil was bad and God was good, African tradition held that these two powers were not mutually exclusive. For, as they knew, the world was not neatly divided into good and bad, but was everywhere both good and bad. Thus, as the anthologizer Newball Niles Puckett states in his book *Folk Beliefs of the Southern Negro:* "One bishop asked them [African Americans] why they persisted in worshipping the devil instead of God. The reply was, 'God is good, God is love and don't hurt anybody—do as you please, God don't hurt you; but do bad and the Devil will get you sure! We not bother about God, but we try to keep on the good side of the Devil.'"

Water was a mystic medium for the African in America. Baptism by water was not only a church experience, but rather a ritual that went back to Africa. One of the best ways to honor a river spirit there was to be possessed by it—to fling oneself into the water and, through immersion, become one with the deity. Obviously, the Baptist church was favored, partly for this reason, by slaves. Also, water rituals aside, many Baptists were poor whites, for whom the slave converts had a certain sympathy. Moreover, the Baptist church was known for its independence and the individual terms with which its parishioners met God.

However, while African-American Baptist practices had similarities to West African rituals, in the West Indies and in South America such religious activities became fully African. The "spiritual Baptist" of Trinidad, for example, sang from the traditional Sankey and Moody hymnal, but as black writer James Haskins has observed: "Markings in white chalk on the floor, at the doors and around the center pole were distinctly African . . . gradually African rhythms would enter in, the tempo would quicken, and

The Ministerial Powers of Daddy Grace. From the Collections of the Library of Congress.

Church Wall, South Chicago. From the Collections of the Library of Congress.

an hour or two after the service had begun it could no longer be called a Baptist service."

Once, some years ago, while attending a Jamaican Neo-Revival church we were struck by the voice of the minister as he spoke in tongues, his eyes rolling back. Accompanying him were a stick-drummer and an electric guitarist. The beat they had fallen upon mimicked the staccato pulsing of the tree frogs in the church-yard. As the congregation fell into a foot-stomping dance, we thought: How African this is! And then, over the palm-fringed hills, we heard the fiercer ring of Kumina drums, and the upraised voices coming from a Kumina church. Those parish-ioners, whose dance was pure possession, were in yet another, even older world. One could sense that the church was unlimit-ed; and that the earth and the sky were part of it. The building was rocking, going up and down and side to side. The church was a woman dancing on a riverbank; the church was a river running uncontained across the land.

CONJURE

The conjure man puts an egg in the road,
a white egg in the road at night.
Then he squeezes lime juice into a porcelain bowl
and mixes in some ashes. He draws a circle
on the earth, and all around it, knives and forks,
upright, sticking out of the leaves. "Come here,"
he says to the man-possessed, and the man comes,
egg-eyed and silent, in a trance.
Now the conjure man peers at his block of amber.
What he sees no one knows. But he draws the
man to him now and pricks his forearm with a
sharp knife. The man's arm bleeds and the blood
runs down. And the conjure man sucks the
bad spirit from the cut on the man's arm
and he spits out pieces of glass, pins, needles,
nails, shells, vials, lizards, spiders, flies,
cat's teeth, snakeskins, fragments of bone;
finally, the conjure man pulls a dead horse,
a rusted-out automobile, a rickety house—and the
man-possessed wakes up and cries, "Mercy!"
— FROM DUPPIES, DRUM TALK & OBEAH MEN,
   BY GERALD HAUSMAN AND RAY GRIFFIN

There are many words that describe the power emanating from earth-objects, fetishes, symbols of magic strength. Among them are mojo, *ouanga (wanga)*, and *grisgris*. Other conjure charms—tricks, jacks, tobies, and luckballs—figure in the spectrum as well, stemming from the crocus bag of hoodoo brought forth by African-American root doctors of the eighteenth and nineteenth centuries. In the 1920s it was speculated that the lore of African fetishism had wrapped itself like a kudzu vine across the Deep South, all the way up to the cotton country of northwestern Oklahoma.

What is conjure?

Conjure is dust and luck, human saliva shining on a copper penny; sulfur fumes and black mushrooms; a charm worn around the neck; a hat worn up on the head. As the Devil says to the legendary black outlaw Stagolee, as he prepares to conscript his soul for eternity:

> *Let's make a deal*
> *and sign it with blood*
> *on a catfish hide*
> *from the Mississippi mud;*
> *Here's a Stetson of oxblood red*
> *made from the skin*
> *of a wildcat's head.*
> *You'll never have to worry*
> *about trouble from the law,*
> *just rub your hat*
> *and give me a call.*
> — FROM "STAGOLEE," BY SID HAUSMAN

The conjure man, traditionally, was a medium between humankind and the Devil, a dealer in darkness whose "goofer bags" (little bundles of charms) were also the special province of root magic, used against illness and disease.

What power the slave had against a tyrannical master was, at best, minimal. Conjure, therefore, could be used for covert revenge or overt violence. Usually, the wielder of this power was a man rather than a woman. The reason is cited by author N. N. Puckett of Chapel Hill:

Because of [their] more limited opportunities for contact with European beliefs in the fields . . . the men clung to the old African beliefs more than the women, who, on the other hand, were more exposed to and influenced by European beliefs in the household; with the result that although women are not excluded, men predominate among Negro conjurers. (FROM MOTHER WIT FROM THE LAUGHING BARREL, *EDITED BY ALAN DUNDES)*

Miss Jenny, a woman of St. Mary, Jamaica, once told me: "Women were as active as men in the practice of witchcraft, but as time went on, the men took over." Perhaps the women were too busy ministering to the young. In any case, herbs, leaves, barks, roots, and seeds were available and useful to either sex. However, of the users of materia medica, perhaps the women were the more devoted practitioners. "The *granny woman* or midwife, the herb woman, and the old woman who has raised a large family to healthy maturity, are the chief practitioners," according to B. A. Botkin's *Treasury of Southern Folklore*. Gloria Naylor opens *Mama Day* with a powerful description of a conjure woman:

Everybody knows but nobody talks about the legend of Sapphira Wade. A true conjure woman: satin black, biscuit cream, red as Georgia clay; depending upon which of us takes a mind to her. She could walk through a lightning storm without being touched; grab a bolt of lightning in the palm of her hand; use the heat of lightning to get the kindling going under her medicine pot; depending on which of us takes a mind to her. She turned the moon into salve, the stars into a swaddling cloth, and healed the wounds of every creature walking up on two or down on four.

"Like cures like," they say, and whether the practitioner is male or female, such notions as "the hair of the dog that bit me" originally came from African proverbs. In today's useage, these phrases mean: To overcome a hangover, one must apply a little more "hair of the dog"—that is, a little bit, but not a lot, of the same alcohol one was drinking the night before.

True conjure, though, means charm, and this often is manifest in the infinite and subtle conjugations of men and women; or, to put it more plainly, the war of the sexes. On the battlefield of love, anything can, and will, happen—not once, but many times over. In the Caribbean islands, the plant called shame-me-lady (a tropic weed that quails when touched) is the same as the one known as shameweed in the American South. They say it will shame a "recalcitrant woman." Sprinkle the powdered dry root in her path and she will close up like a sensitive plant. Mix it with snail dust and snail water and she will withdraw like a snail going into its shell. Women's conjure works its way into the minds of men in the same manner; to get rid of a love rival, put the name in some ashes and let the chickens pick at it; dry the heart of a hummingbird and sprinkle the powder on whom you desire; wrap a thimble in a small piece of silk and carry it in your pocket for three days. The *grisgris*, or magical charm, for a future marriage is to join the hands of two dolls with a ribbon. Then make a mound of sand into which you place nine wax candles. Sprinkle the dolls and candles with champagne, while saying, "St. Joseph, make this marriage and I'll pay." Payment, while the marriage is taking place, is a plate of macaroni and parsley set out for the saint.

In all conjure, good and bad and the variable grayness in between, the netherworld between nadir and zenith, there is an unequivocal grasp of the symbol. The gods and goddesses of ancient Africa live not in the ether but in the material world, in physical fact. Thus the wine, the rum, the syrup, and the salt. Such things all have equivalents in the spirit world—flesh is moved by them, and, in the case of conjure, deliberately manipulated. A blood baptism, or purification ritual, for an adult on the island of Haiti involves the incorporeal beings that watch over the earth

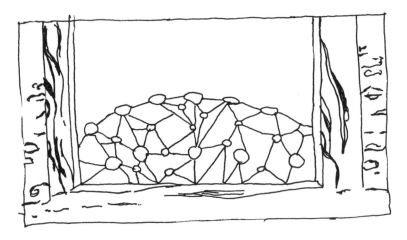

Haitian Vaudou Threshold Motif *(to ward off "unwelcome forces")*. From *The Magic Island* by William Seabrook.

and the invocation of the earth itself. So the immaterial, as always, is plotted and placed and substantiated upon the material. William Seabrook in *The Magic Island*:

> When this singing and pouring of libations were ended, the papaloi sealed the open doorway by tracing thus across its earthen sill.
> Evil or unwelcome forces which sought to enter would become entangled in the lines and go wandering from circle to circle like lost souls among the stars. . . .
> The papaloi took from the altar an egg which had surmounted a little pyramid of cornmeal, and holding it aloft in his cupped hands, pronounced incantations. As the blood had represented the mystery of death, sacrifice and purification, likewise fertilization as it was poured upon the earth, the egg now represented rebirth, productivity, fertility, re-creation.

This ritual of darkness shares something of a soul-retrieving effect with Navajo sand paintings whose intent is to bring forth the goodness of the gods—to let them enter upon the symbolic sand of creation, to re-create the health of the patient. Afterward, the ceremony completed, the sacred sand is offered to all who might wish to sprinkle it on their own ailing body parts. It then is returned to the winds and to Mother Earth.

Such was the power of hair, salt, sulfur, and mustard seed that all conjure men and women used them to work cures and to stagger opponents. If, for example, on waking you found a little four-holed acorn stuffed with the hair of a dead person, and two small chicken feathers drawn through to make a cross at the foot of your bed, you would know someone had it in for you. *Grisgris* charms against this maleficence would be the little red bags containing powdered brick, yellow ocher, and cayenne pepper; these were the countercharm returned by another conjurer to the one who meant to do you harm. This story of the infamous nineteenth-century vaudou priestess Marie Laveau appeared in the *New Orleans Times-Picayune*:

A certain young man in New Orleans, many years ago, had been arrested in connection with a crime, and though his companions were in reality the guilty ones, the blame was laid upon his shoulders. The grief-stricken father immediately sought Marie Laveau, explaining to her the circumstances of the case, and offered her a handsome reward if she would obtain his son's release. When the day set for the trial came round, Marie Laveau, after placing three guinea peppers in her mouth, entered the St. Louis Cathedral, knelt at the altar rail, and was seen to remain in this posture for some time. Leaving the church, she gained admittance to the Cabildo where the trial was to be held, and depositing three of the same peppers under the judge's bench, lingered to wait for developments. After a lengthy deliberation, though the evidence seemed unfavorable to the prisoner, the jury finally made its report. The judge was heard to pronounce the words "not guilty."

However, in love and war, in hatred and revenge, there comes a time when no power is greater, no *grisgris* more potent than the simple conjure of humor. The war club–wielding Congo priestess in *A Woman Named Solitude* asks a question to an assembly of runaway slaves like herself:

"Sometimes I wonder why God created the White man, and it plagues me, here in my big head. . . ."

Everyone laughed at the question that was plaguing her and at her way of speaking. And one of the men answered briskly, for the saltwater folk hold that a man's tongue is made to be used: "Dear woman, don't blame God for creating the tiger . . . thank him for not giving him wings. . . ."

Whereupon everyone present laughed loudly, conjuring the ever-present spirits of Camaraderie and Goodness, two angels who know that when people laugh, Danger withdraws.

COWRIES

The desert and the sea came together one day
    when you gave me heishi nine years ago.
I said, "That is a fine shell-choker," and you took
    it from your neck, and that was that: you handed
    it over, Navajo-style.
Then, you showed up again. "'Nice necklace," you said,
    pointing to a string of Antiguan cowries I was wearing.
    "Fine," I said, "here you are," returning
    nine cowries for the nine-year loan of heishi.
"This is what is meant by Indian-giving," you told me,
putting the cowries around your neck. It is nine years
since I saw you last, walking out into the desert sun
like an African legend. "Heishi and cowries come
to the same thing," you said, the copper sea sparkling
in your eyes, hinting at what my heart hinted at:
we are one; and I hope they brought you luck.
— FROM "NIGHT IN THE WEST INDIES," BY GERALD HAUSMAN

Background: African Dance Belt with Cowry Shells. Photograph by Bobbe Besold.

The harp shell, the painted snail, the angel's wing, the triangular trumpet—all colorful shells from the sparkling islands of the "Golden Lake," the Caribbean, each a kind of stone fort built by a mollusk to provide protection. From the gland of a mollusk, then, come the sundance patterns of the leopard cowrie, so named for the dazzle of dark spots on a cream gloss skin of marble hue. Consisting largely of carbonate of lime—the same substance, essentially, of which the Caribbean islands are made—shells are formed of more or less equal proportions of limestone, chalk, and marble.

Leopard Cowry Shell. Photograph by Bobbe Besold.

Belts of wampum made of cowrie shells may have their contemporary corollary in today's money belt. During the sixteenth century, shell belts were traded and used as money by coastal Native American tribes who bartered with their inland brothers. The most widely used "money shell" throughout the Americas, the West Indies, and Africa was the cowrie. The ringed cowrie, in fact, was used on remote Indian and Pacific islands well into the 1950s. Along the west coast of Africa, strings of money cowrie were standard currency until past the middle of the nineteenth century. A seventeenth-century English writer, describing the contents of two trade ships in London harbor, was surprised to find their holds laden with "curious little shells of the African Coast." Culturally, shells have always represented, among indigenous peoples, the sign of a prosperous journey. This favorable implication arises partially from the shell's association with water, the source of fertility as well as their moon-shaped, womanly form. Cowries were often used as adornment—earrings, necklaces, belts, and vest covers. The abeng, an African conch shell, whose significance and name come from Africa, was once the trumpet of rebellion, used by the Maroon scouts to signal their armies in the bush. A musical language developed around this instrument, which was, because of its signaling power, comparable to the drum. The abeng played a significant role in William Golding's novel *Lord of the Flies*. The call of the conch became, in the minds of the islanded boys, a call to reason, a signal of cooperation and order within the chaos of internecine war.

Within the fluted shape of the shell, there is the voice of eternal time, the great mother ocean. The sound of the sea echoes in the elliptical, earlike interior of the shell. And its shape was considered "an ear extended outward to the universe," hearing all, and combining—in its texture like the rolling of a wave—the presence of all universal sound, the East Indian "Om."

African Dance Belt. Photograph by Bobbe Besold.

Once, right after the ravages of Hurricane Gilbert, we delivered relief funds to a community on the north coast of Jamaica. It was but a token, but it helped with the painful task of rebuilding what was lost, and it gave one small village some precious hope during a difficult time. One moonlit night, when the sea seemed to be minting silver coins in the shallows of the bay, a barefooted man came to us and said, "No one should give and not receive. I have no money, but I have these." He opened a box on the grass and in the clear moonlight presented us with money-cowrie. Pleasurably, he jingled the box to show that it rang like money, that it had been saved and stored like clinking coin, and was, above all, his family treasure.

"Take one of these money-cowrie for each member of your family," the man offered generously. We selected four moon-burned shells that felt good in the palm. He smiled. "The loan is paid."

"But it wasn't a loan," we told him. "It was a gift from the people of our village to the people of yours."

He looked thoughtful then; his face furrowed.

"I don't got enough cowrie for a whole village," he said in dismay.

We told him, "We didn't raise enough money for yours either."

But for a long while thereafter, one shell for each year that passed, he made his annual contribution, a gleaming cowrie, brightening our doorstep every August afternoon, interest paid on a non–interest bearing note of friendship.

I have heard the sea on summer nights
jealously counting her change
The shuffle and shake of coinage—
communion of moon and mollusk
in the compression of tide and time.
The little pebble-rustle as the crisp salt retreats
with claws of lace; the mingling of crabs,
black-footed, spidery, over coconut fronds.
And I have seen whelk gatherers on shark-toothed
rocks with lustreless butter-knives
Carving out a meal
while pocketing the sea-pretties
cast up around their toes.
Taking a free meal
and saving money-cowrie at the same time;
ah, the sea that so richly rewards
offers now a severed hand, ribboned with weed,
the mouths of tiny starfish pressed to the wrist
where, still ticking, there clings a battered Bulova watch.
—FROM "NIGHT IN THE WEST INDIES," BY GERALD HAUSMAN

DOG

The African mythology of the canine begins with the animal-headed gods of Egypt. Anubis, dog-headed and jackallike, was by no means a deified animal, but the god manifest in the grave-haunting dog or jackal. God of desert cemeteries, of embalming, of burial. It must have come as no surprise, therefore, to the runaways, the Maroons of America and the West Indies, that their nemesis was to be the creature of legend they brought with them from Africa. On the island of Jamaica, the Maroons proved invincible, so elusive in their jungle hideaways, their swampy seclusions, that the Earl of Balcarres and his council decided to use dogs:

A shipload of 100 of these terrifying beasts was imported from Cuba, where they were in common use for hunting runaway slaves and robbers. . . . The news of the dogs' arrival caused a panic among the Maroons. In the wild and uncharted Cockpit Country, the Maroons had shown that they could elude almost any number of troops sent against them; but there was no escape from savage bloodhounds that tracked by scent. Before the dogs could be released against them, the Trelawnys [Maroons] sued for peace. (FROM JAMAICA/INSIGHT GUIDES)

However, it must be noted that it was not the dogs themselves that subdued the fierce African guerrilla fighters; it was the idea of them, the intangible legend of an old death threat. In Dahoman myth, the dog was the messenger of Legba, the divine trickster. It was Legba who conferred upon the canine the attributes of divinity. Dog thus became the guardian of women, the leader of all spirits, and the leader of all men who are lost. The power of Dog was, therefore, infallible. And it is no accident that the ear-to-ear mouths of the squatting red clay figurines of Legba are always given dog teeth.

The origin of the dog's mouth appears in the African-American Gullah story wherein God observes that whenever he eats, Dog's eyes follow him from hand to spoon to mouth. So he gives Dog a mouth. The other animals then crowd around, seeing that Dog can eat, and carry a stick, and do other marvelous things with mouth and teeth. If he gets a thorn between the toes, he can bite it out; if he wants to clean his fur, he can use his tongue and teeth to do so. The animals pray to God to have mouths of their own, but it is Dog himself who acts as ambassador in their behalf, going to God and saying: "Give them mouths, Master." And God, though uneasy about the effects of this act, does, in the end, confer mouths upon the other members of the animal world.

The Nyanga people of what is now Zaire tell how the first dog bestowed fire upon man, and soon after became a skilled and indispensable hunter. However, as the story evolves around Dog's usefulness to man, it is also understood that Dog is too fast for man to keep up with on the hunt. Therefore, Dog devises a bell to wear around his neck so that his master will always hear him coming or going, and so that he will always know where Dog has gone. This bell—precursor, perhaps, to dog chain and tag—was a piece of magic wood, a little bone with a hard covering of antelope skin. The hunting culture of most of central Africa celebrates the cooperation of man and dog and the little collar bell that unites them.

In the tidewater region of Virginia, the hunting rites of Africa reemerged with the freed slaves there, who raised dogs for hunting coon and possum. It took a very smart hound to hunt the clever coon, who, in African American myth, "had learned to box

Background: Hunters with Dogs. Rock Painting, North Africa. From *God Had a Dog* by Maria Leach.

by sparring with lightning." Unlike the Nyanga dogs, which were barkless, coonhounds had, and have, a baleful cry that their owners call "giving mouth." The precise timbre of the dog's voice indicates to the hunter whether the coon is "on the run" or whether a "cold scent has been struck." When the dogs are on the run, the baying is openmouthed and prolonged. When they're up close to the quarry, their voices become short, sharp, and anxious. When the coon is finally treed, only one dog in the pack gives mouth; the others bay slowly, as if listening between each breath for the hunter's response.

Dog duality—the so-called split-dog myth—may, in fact, derive from the origin tales of Egypt and Africa. Congolese shamans still make fetishes that present two-headed dogs as intermediaries between life and death. In the African-American split-dog stories, the dog itself is severed into twoness, but it does not die. Hence, in the North Carolina tale of the fast rabbit dog that ran into a tree, cut himself in two, and was put back together again by his master, the animal takes well to his new condition: "two feet up and two feet down." As the story unfolds, the dog runs as long as it can on two feet, then rolls over and runs on the equally nimble other two.

Mark Twain, in his antislavery novel *Pudd'nhead Wilson*, has his protagonist comment on a dog that is always barking: "I wish I owned half of that dog," Wilson remarks. When his listener wonders why, Wilson returns wryly, "I'd kill my half." According to sources from the early nineteenth century, the myth of the split dog may be one of America's earliest folktales.

The folk song "Salty Dog" uses the venerable image of man-and-dog-in-duality in yet another way; here, the dog becomes an expression of love, in which a woman enters into the picture:

Salty Dog, Salty Dog
I don't want to be your man at all;
Honey, let me be your Salty Dog.

Songs of praise are sung all over Africa, but among the Hausa, dog songs take the following turn: a spicy duality, a celebration of the dog's thinness, the many beatings he receives, and his ability to cancel a prayer if his shadow falls upon one who is in the act of prayer:

O Dog, your breakfast is a club!
O Dog, your ribs are like the plaits in a grass mat!
O Dog, you spoil a prayer!
O Dog, your nose is always moist!

Ultimately, it is the dog's commonly known usefulness, as the ancient guardian of women, that African-American and West Indian people venerate and build their myths around. In Jamaica, the story is told thus:

A man caller came to see a woman.
The woman's dog barked so loud, the man went away.
So the woman burned up the dog.
The next day when the man came again, the ashes in the cookfire barked.
So the woman dumped the ashes in the river.
The next day when the man came again, the river barked.
So the woman gathered up the ashes in the river and dumped them in the sea.
The dog barked no more, and when next the man came to call, he caught the woman in his arms and tore her up into tiny little pieces.

DRUM

Old Drum, I hear you, do you know?
Old soft skin, so near, so far, I hear you.
The sound of children's voices
droning verses; pigeons under eaves
cooing, the clicking of claws
on roof tiles. A priest chanting; through the
arched doorway, sunlight pouring.
Old Drum, my redeemer, I hear you
above all others. You, alone, speak
my language—boom-boom-badoom —
echoing on the cobbles of Congo Square.
No one knows, Old Drum, what you say
but I am sweating, listening
to your words, Old Drum. Your words
telling me that the hour of Africa has come,
When we hear you, we shall fly away
like pigeons and children's
voices-verses that straighten up in the air
and drift away over field and wood
and across the sea, like a dream —
Old Drum, do you know that I, too,
was born in Africa?
— *BY GERALD HAUSMAN/KELVIN RODRIQUES*

The high tympanic bell-blows of the repeater drum with the skin
stretched tight as ice. Hear it. Ta-ping, ta-ping. The hard fingers
coming down like guava sticks. And, once again: drub-bub, drub-

Steel Drummer. Photograph by
Barbara Baumann.

bub. The whole hand, laid out like a fat frog on a lily pad, croak-
ing like a happy heart.

How can one drum make so many sounds? How can it make
the forest breathe through the roots and through the green flags
of wind-rushed leaves and through the boles and blossoms of the
cotton tree?

In *Our Grandmother's Drums,* Mark Hudson explores the cultural assimilation necessary for understanding the true motif of the African drum.

Unlike in the West, where the beating of drums is used largely as an accompaniment to melody, in Africa it is not seen as music as we understand the word. The rhythms are inextricably bound up in the rituals and processes of the people's lives. And like these processes, their forms are precise, and prescribed. Two rhythms which, to a European, may sound equally precise, meaningful and satisfying, may be, to an African, as different as a well-honed sentence and a stream of gibberish. If it is not one of the traditional rhythms of their culture, it is nothing. They don't even hear it as a rhythm.

They say the drum is the voice of God given to man so that he might speak in tones of godliness. It is made, let us say, from the tall tree of the world and from the lowly hide of the goat. Bowl-shaped, earthly in nature, the drum makes the sound of the heart. And the fingers of man are the tongues that touch the palate of the drum so that it can speak for everyone.

THE SKIN
First the goat
must be killed
and the skin
stretched.

Bless you, four-footed animal, who eats rope,
skilled
upon rocks, horned with our sin;
stretch your skin, stretch

it tight on our hope;
we have killed
you to make a thin
voice that will reach

further than hope
further than heaven, that will
reach deep down to our gods where the thin
light cannot leak, where our stretched

hearts cannot leap. . . .
— FROM "THE MAKING OF THE DRUM," BY EDWARD BRATHWAITE

We witnessed once the killing of a goat, saw the outstretched
front legs as on a cross, the goat crucified to become a drum. Its
cries were in the skin when the drum was played, and we were
told by the drum-maker: "That is the woman goat that makes so
high a cry." We came to understand that only the thin skin of the
female goat, cured in sun and rubbed with ash, could carry the
sound of such crying. This was, we learned, the African repeater
drum—the one that sounded like the tin cans the fabled goat was
supposed to eat.

Another time at a revival church, singing songs of Jesus, in the
lull between preacher and prayer, song and shout, we heard
drumming fill the valley, the hills echoing with it: Kumina drums.
They rose and fell with the spirit of the wind and, though the
preacher sought to overpower them with microphone and organ,
the Kumina drums overcame him. The name "Kumina" seems to
be of Bantu origin. *Kumina,* a drum sound itself, meaning "to
move or act rhythmically." Also *kumu,* "to mount up," which, in
fact, the Kumina drummer does. Straddling his drum, mounting
it, he beats out a fierce tribal rhythm that is designed to draw
forth the ancestors of sky, earth, and underworld.

The kbandu, a large hollow drum with a goatskin at one end,
takes firm control while scrapers, shakers, and catta sticks play a
game of come and go, attack and run. As the wild rhythms chase
each other, the dancers become possessed by spirits and, as in
vaudou ceremony, they are thus "mounted by the gods," and then
ridden into ecstasy.

The Shona people of Zimbabwe, Africa, express the power of

Akete Drummer. Photograph by
Bobbe Besold.

the drum as necessity, and as cultural urgency. The following
tale and excerpts on Shona culture were collected by drum student Seth Cohen. It was told by storyteller Ephat Mujuru in
Zimbabwe.

*There were once three hunters, one who was extremely talented.
One day, when the three men were out in the forest, an animal went
into the trunk of a very large tree. The skilled hunter followed the
animal there. The other hunters, who were jealous of the first, barri-
caded the entrance of the trunk, closing the hunter in.*

*The villagers were unaware of what had happened, and they
assumed the man had been eaten by a wild animal. But then, one
day, a man went to the forest to make a drum, and he chose that
same tree. As he was chopping—"ngo, ngo, ngo"—(the sound of the*

axe hitting the tree), the trapped hunter said, "Chiya chati hgo chiyi ngo?"—What is it making that sound?

The man chopping the tree also began to feel a strange rhythm as he chopped. When he returned to the village, he told the people about the special tree he had found. After a while, the villagers went there and they all began singing to the rhythm: "Chiya chati ngo chiyi ngo. Chiya chati ngo idanda"—What is it that is making that sound, the trunk of the tree?

Now, when the people stopped singing, they heard a humming, and they investigated the tree, and found the trapped hunter. The hunter was filled with joy and thankful for the drum because it had brought the drum-maker to him, and then the villagers. The drum was the reason the man went to chop the tree. And it was the rhythm of the drum, produced by the axe falling on the hollow wood, that brought the villagers to find him as well.

Is it the spirit of the drum, or the drum's spirit set loose in a man, that makes the instrument so powerful, so ripe with magic? A *conun-drum*, then: "Can a dreamer dream a drum, or a drummer drum a dream?" It is said there is a drum sound in the very word itself—a word-heart with a beat. The Shona word *ngoma*, drum, has an ancestor sound, as do the players, *muridzi we ngoma*.

Sekuru Dzapasi, a drummer from Zimbabwe, explains that when he plays the drums, he feels possessed by a forefather who was once a drummer. Wearing his skirt of animal skins and his headdress, he says, "is like a soldier putting on a uniform, to carry out this duty." But, when he is playing, he becomes a coordinator between the two worlds, the living and the dead: "The drums please the mudzimu, the spirits. They communicate with them before possession. Once this happens, and possession takes over, I stop playing *ngoma*."

The feeling that the drum lives not as an instrument of man

but as an independent entity with man as the keeper was expressed to me by drummer Tony Delmohamid:

We were singing songs in the moonlight when Tony reminded us that our drums were thirsty. "You cannot play a drum without giving it a little drink, now and then," he said. Then he poured some dark rum on the goatskin head, rubbing the rum around the drum's rim and across the surface of the taut skin.

Another drummer, Kofi, expressed it thus:

What are the first notes a drummer learns? Mama, papa. Mama, papa. Tap, tap; tap, tap. Like a chicken coming out of an egg. The first words the drum speaks are the first notes the drummer learns, just like the child, who only knows two words, the only words he needs to stay alive, Mama, Papa.

Drum speaks; yes, the drum speaks in many tongues.

The tongues of many nations, all touching the same rim of mouth, all uttering the deep boomalay-boom of the heart, all searching for the word, the one word given by God in the beginning.

DUPPY

The duppy is a West Indian ghost, also known as a jumbie. A common theme in West Indian folklore, the duppy is sometimes thought to be harmless, but most often is regarded as an evil spirit. Duppies, along with a myriad of other supernatural beings, have the ability to "dream you." This means they can enter a person's sleep and direct thoughts to him; or, worse, they can steal away the "small soul." Most traditional West Indian people believe that there are two souls: the small soul, which is somewhat playful and roams about at night when you sleep, thus being, temporarily open to "duppy attack"; and the large soul, which is part of the physical structure, as they say, until death, when it becomes a part of nature, a part of the earth. It is the large soul, then, that holds a potential danger because it can be manipulated after death, and can become, depending on the circumstances of death or the will of the manipulator, an evil entity.

Long ago, shadow catchers were those who, mostly for the purpose of good, could trap a duppy by calling it out of the silk-cotton tree where it had taken up residence. Another way of trapping it was to confound it; for instance, it was thought that a duppy couldn't move when the shadow catcher drew a figure eight in the dirt and placed a knife blade in the heart, or center of it. Some say duppies like salt; others say they do not. In any case, it was once possible to entrap a duppy by throwing salt in its face; also by asking it to count to ten (duppies, according to folk belief, can only count to five, whereupon they stall out, and go back to one).

There are hundreds of superstitions revolving around duppies. One is that duppies often reside in the body of an animal, usually a dog or a crab. To view a duppy—they are not always easy to see—one boils rice and rinses the eyes in the grayish residue; this will enable one to see a duppy. A more repugnant way is to rub a dog's eye-matter in one's own eyes, for it is believed that dogs see duppies better than people do. Birds associated with duppies are the chick-mon-chick-bird; patoo, the owl; the gimme-me-bit; and the ground dove. Plants, too, share in duppy lore. The spineless cactus called tuna is planted at the four corners of a field as a duppy guard; the overlook bean is planted for the same purpose; and the duppy gun is a seed pod that explodes in water, and is thus also referred to as duppy-fly-away.

Duppies come in many enchanting shapes and sizes. There is the rolling calf with fire-coal eyes and clanking chains that falls down hills, throwing off balls of fire as it rolls. There is the old hige, or hag, the witch who removes her skin and becomes an owl at night. (To put an end to her, you must salt and pepper her shed skin, so that she will reject it when she finds it at dawn.) The river mumma is another duppylike creature, the combination of the African rivermaid and the Celtic mermaid; she is the powerful figure of the revival cults, and sacrifices are made for her at the river mouth or spring where she is said to live.

At a revival gathering that we attended, a sacred baptismal spring, said to be inhabited by the river mumma, had dried up. The shadow catcher killed a chicken, scattered its blood in a circle around the spring, then sprayed mouthfuls of white rum. He then recited a few verses from the Old Testament, and told everyone to leave the place for twenty-four hours.

We asked him what had happened to the spring water.

"Someone abused the water spirit," he explained. "You see, she has the tail of a fish, the head and body of a woman. She has gold hair, dark skin the color of St. Ann's honey. Her little children, small freshwater fish, spin around her head, and she always asks those who come to take a drink if they like fresh or salt. This means, do they eat freshwater or saltwater fish. If the passerby says 'fresh,' the river mumma drowns him on the spot, but if he says 'salt,' she lets him drink the spring water. The story goes back to an Arawak chief whose golden treasure was guarded by a river mumma. A Spanish explorer tried to steal her golden comb, and she drowned him. That was how it all began."

We asked the man if he believed the story was true, and he answered that there were people in the village, notably an old man named Sweet Sweet, who had seen the river mumma when he was a young man and was still talking about it. It was not much trouble to find Sweet Sweet and ask him to tell the story, which he willingly did, adding some savory details about the mumma's anatomy. He kept repeating that her head was "big-big," way out of proportion to her body, which, though beautiful, was odd next to that off-sized head. This was partly what made her terrifying, he told us. He also added the fact that she had been around a long, long time and guarded the sacred streams of the Arawak Indians. When asked why the mumma was so frightening, he raised his eyebrows and practically blew steam in our faces: "She an evil spirit," he resounded, "she kill you."

Everyone, it seems, has a duppy story to share, if you have the time to listen. One of our favorites is the tale of the cab driver who, driving home late at night, picks up two little girls by the side of the road. They are wearing white nightdresses. He takes them to a house, which they say belongs to their grandmother, at the top of a steep, jungly hill. When he gets there, the old woman comes out to the veranda with a kerosene lamp to greet them. He drives home, thinking nothing further about this until the following day, when he is told that the house on the hill burned down some years before; an old granny living there with her two grand-daughters caught the place on fire by upsetting a kerosene lamp. All three had burned to death.

Another duppy tale was told during a drum ceremony. We were told by the drum master that our drums were "thirsty" and need-ed a drink. A bottle of white rum was produced and passed around; each drummer poured a libation on the head of his drum. Then the drum master took the bottle and poured some white rum into the earth. "This drink of rum," he explained, "is for our departed friend, Raoul, who drowned a few weeks ago." He then went on to say that at the very hour that Raoul was drowned, he, the drum master, was diving at a nearby beach searching for gray pearls.

Jamaican Rolling Calf Duppy. Rendering from a 19th century engraving by Mariah Fox.

Suddenly he felt a hand take hold of his wrist. At first he resisted it; then he heard his friend Raoul say, "Do not be afraid, my friend, I am going to help you." The voice came from within his inner ear. He could not doubt that it was Raoul, for he knew the timbre of his voice, and this was undoubtedly it. So, overcoming his fear, he allowed the pull on his wrist to tighten and take him out toward the reef. There on the white sand he saw a huge sea oyster with its pink, pulpy mouth open to the outgoing tide. Quickly, he dove down and saw the largest gray pearl he had ever seen. Half the size of his fist, it lay in the pink folds of skin, radiating beauty.

"That pearl," he concluded, "helped buy my house and start my jewelry business."

"What about the voice and the tug on your wrist?" he was asked.

"That," he said, "was the duppy of my childhood friend Raoul. He took me to that pearl; it was the last thing he did after he died."

"Then, the duppies aren't always evil spirits?"

"No, mon," he replied, "duppies can be anything we dream them to be . . . or we can be anything they dream us to be. You see, the spirit world is not separate from ours. They live partly in our world; we live partly in theirs. It is just so."

ELEPHANT

I saw the elephants today
The elephants they move as one
So Africa should live as one.

I saw the elephants today
Side of Africa, side by side
Move up, move up Africa
Move up as one.

I saw the elephants today
And they were defending each other
Why can't east, west, north and south Africa
Stand up as one?
— FROM MEK WE DWEET, *BY BURNING SPEAR*

Moving as one, a group of elephants lifted the body of their slain friend and family member, and in the moonlight and under the watchful eyes of men, carried him through the maize and into the forest, where they preserved his spirit with a moonlit vigil. Elephants have been known to carry off the whitened bones of a relative in the same way, or to pull out, with their powerful trunks, the tusks of one killed for its ivory. Isak Dinesen said, "In the very old days the elephant, upon the roof of the earth, led an existence deeply satisfying to himself and fit to be set up as an example to the rest of creation." Yet, as humankind moves laboriously into the twenty-first century, the grand old elephant, with its great gray ears like flags of doom, speaks to us from another time. As poet Ross LewAllen expresses it in his "Poem for Elephants":

Some of the coals were gray-green
Some were still smoldering
It smelled of burnt bone
burnt flesh, burnt horn.

They put varnish on the bones
so they would burn.
130 million dollars-worth
of ivory on the foreign trade market

I closed my eyes
let some of the ashes
sift through my fingers
Did the poachers see the flames?

Mother Elephant and Calf. Photograph by Ross LewAllen.

And does the elephant, moving as one, ever take revenge, in the sense that we know it? Julian, of Lake Victoria: "The best they do is maybe they gore you with their ivory, they break you into pieces, and then into small pieces again, and then they look down and they just trample again until you are dust; that's when they give up." Writer George Adamson disagrees with the thesis that the elephant ever gives up. After killing a man, trampling and goring him repeatedly, and spading the thirty square feet of earth where the killing took place, "every afternoon since the tragedy, the elephant had returned to the spot, and stood there until evening." Adamson's conviction is that there is an evident brotherhood of elephant and man, going back to time immemorial, as long as an elephant's memory and as short as man's ability to see into the future. That the elephant is a thing of permanence, however, is cited in a Nama tale wherein an elephant marries a Nama woman, who, in true human fashion, runs out on him. He pursues; she comes to a great rock, and can go no farther.

"Rock of my forefathers," she pleads, "spread out to both sides for us."

The rock parts then, and closes after she has gone through. When the elephant comes along, seeking his wife, he, too, asks the rock to cleave, and it does. However, when he enters and tries to pass through, the massive rock closes, imprisoning him. As the tale demonstrates, a permanent sorrow seems to hang about the elephant. He is stone; he is grief; he is love unrequited. And, going about his business, which is simple enough, he meets, on the mythic plane, human greed in equal proportion to his own magnificent size.

Perhaps, as some legends tell us, he is the close relation of death, the true gray eminence. On the other hand, it could be that his chief and most accentuated virtue, patience, is somewhat despised in a world that moves hastily along, like the hyena, chasing its own ragged tail. The elephant cannot see its tail; it must, as the proverb recounts, move ever forward into the indefinite future, blending with the low-lying clouds, of which it is a herd member.

Some say the real voice of the elephant, not its trumpet blast, is an infrasound, below the range of human hearing. It is strange to think of anything so large as an elephant being in the select company of bats and shrews, but there you have it: An elephant sends messages, high-frequency sounds that travel over great distances. It's been estimated that such communication can travel up to six miles.

For elephants, the unity of the family is everything; and the family is matrilineal—mothers, daughters, sisters, working together as one, moving up as one. The bulls remain, it would seem, aloof, as is their nature. But the females, whose workaday tasks are never done, live within the boundaries of nurturing care. These matriarchal families, from all reports, are extremely stable and well-ordered.

Imagine the tip of the trunk of the elder matriarch, who, encountering an eight-year-old girl child for the first time, smelled her; and smelled her, drawing in her essence. The question of the elephant, then, is like Samson's riddle of the lion—how can something so strong emanate so palpable a sweetness? It is this that has adapted the elephant, over the aeons, for life on an essentially barbaric planet, one where, as the saying goes, "might makes right." In deliberately choosing not to assert its prerogative of violent strength, the elephant remains cloudlike, impeccable, misunderstood by what e. e. cummings called "manunkind."

ELEPHANT
I watched a mother elephant
gently lay her tusk
over the back
of her baby
She carefully moved her trunk
from the left side
to the right side
of the baby's body
I felt the powerful sense
of touch at work
Dusty gray
moving in the night
Kilimanjaro's healing water
fills their favorite swamp
The elephant's night pace
is tranquil
—ROSS LEWALLEN

FATHER

What are the boundaries of our Father's love?
His love is limitless, created of continuous bliss.
Can we also express love?
Yes, if we accept limitless love,
Then we can experience continuous bliss.
— KELVIN RODRIQUES

The Father. Drawing by Teri Sanders, Kansas City Art Institute.

Some years ago, our West Indian friend Mackie, whose Ashanti teaching came from his grandmother, a bush doctor in the Jamaican parish of St. Ann, taught us a very valuable lesson. We would look at his face and imagine that he was a mask: He could see out, but no one could see in. No matter how hot it was, Mackie was always ineffably cool. We watched him swim out of shadow into light, and back into shadow again. Darkness was his medium. He liked night so much that even during the day, he seemed to move about invisibly.

Somehow we knew that our time together was going to be brief. It turned out that it was, indeed, momentary. We had become brothers, in the true sense of the word, and suddenly Mackie went behind the clouds once and for all—felled by an illness that neither of us would ever fully understand. But our time together was sacred, whether striding in and out of the Trenchtown ghetto in Kingston, or jogging through the bushy hills of Highgate, the mountain town where Oliver Cromwell was once exiled.

Of all the stories of Mackie, we like this one best, for it happened exactly as told here. It illustrates, among other things, the absolute measure with which the concept of Father as Sun, Spirit, Guardian, Deity is universally African. As Mackie makes clear, there is no escaping either the Father or Fatherhood. In either case, a man proves himself a man by knowing that he is one with the Father and so, one with himself.

One afternoon Mackie was sitting with his son, Junior, under a casuarina tree. His knees were up, his face directed toward Cabarita Island. Above him the feathery limbs soughed in the wind. Below him the sea coughed shells on the cobble beach where there lay a long, frosted aluminum cylinder. On the side of it was stamped in bold black letters the warning: "Danger! Incendiary Explosive. Property of the United States Navy. If recovered, report at once to military authorities."

It looked exactly like what it appeared to be: a bomb. Mackie stared disconsolately at the cylinder for a long time. Finally, he got up and, seeing a boy riding a bicycle on the road nearby, he called out:

"Boy! Me find one of them bombs. Tell police come here, quick!"

A shrill voice cried—"Yah, mon!" and the bicycle boy sailed down the hill to Port Maria.

Mackie and Junior both reacted to the bomb in the same way, with an instantaneous neutrality. But it wasn't long before they began to speak about it in that peculiarly Jamaican style known as "reasoning."

"Look at that palm tree there," Mackie said, "that palm dead, you know."

The old wind-warped, hill-crawling palm appeared lifeless; its dead fronds hung like soiled rags, its trunk was sickly gray. But climbing up its length was a pretty yellow creeper, a vine that was called a wiss in Jamaica.

"The wiss is dead," Junior remarked, initiating a reasoning session.

"Not yet. But the palm reach his destiny," Mackie answered.

Then he chuckled and asked his son: "What thing most pretty, that old dead palm, or the new vine that dead it?"

The vine was one of those tropical stranglers; by definition, a large dangerous weed—something that kills, and is therefore especially worthy of being killed. Yet, in the fading light, the vine's leaves were poetry to the eye. Mackie's point was obvious: The vine's deathly beauty had transcended the once-beautiful palm tree.

"The vine prettier," Junior said flatly.

"This bomb, this thing that mosh we up . . . What prettier—Jamaica, or the cloud of smoke in the sky after Jamaica's all gone?"

"Jamaica." Junior cocked his head, wondering what his father was driving at.

Mackie squinted back, questioning his son's questioning.

"You never see the bomb blow—how can you say?"

"I *see* Jamaica *now*," Junior said.

"From high up where the Father sees all things, this bomb of death could mean life." Then, sighing, Mackie added, "Strangle-vine—pretty, pretty," shaking his head, smiling.

Junior asked, "So you think death is pretty?"

"All things come from the Father," Mackie said serenely.

"The bomb is from the devil," Junior said, his voice rising defiantly.

"All things come from the Father."

"How can you say this devil-bomb is the Father's?"

"All things come from the Father," Mackie repeated.

"What's the use?" Junior said, shrugging.

"No, mon." Mackie grinned. "Me say, 'All things come from the Father' 'cause me know it's true; it's inna me *heart*, not just inna me *head*."

The reasoning session was interrupted by the groan of a four-wheel vehicle coming up the road. A Land Cruiser nosed its square grille into the gateway. Four well-groomed officers of Jamaican law stepped out, their dark blue pants with the side

Roy McKay, Castle Gordon, Port Maria, Jamaica. Photograph by Frank Bond.

stripe of crimson crisply pressed, their pinstripe short-sleeved shirts ironed and new. They squatted down, in unison, and inspected the bomb from a distance of about three feet.

They appeared to be meditating on the bomb, but every so often, their eyes would stray away toward Cabarita Island and the little spit of land on top of the reef known as Hurricane Allen Point. Mackie's eyes went from the bomb, to the officers, to the vine and its progress up the length of the dying palm.

After a while, he asked: "So what you gwine do wid dis ting?"

The senior officer, a handsome man in his early twenties with a small mustache and a heavy face, cleared his throat.

"You carry come down a station," he said.

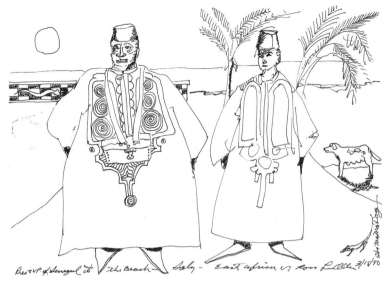

"What the mon seh fe do?" Mackie asked one of the other officers.

This man, looking sleepily away, shrugged his shoulders.

The other officer said, "Mon seh you tek that thing, and bring it down de station house."

"Me?" Mackie said, doubtfully. "No me work dis—"

The senior officer turned scornfully to Mackie.

"You listen me, mon," he said, "You see dat bwai?"

The same small boy on the battered bicycle who had summoned the police cautiously wheeled his way into their midst.

"Me see de bwai," Mackie answered.

"You give him de bomb tek fe military. No police job dis."

The boy's mouth fell open.

"Me ride alla way to military wid dis bomb on me back?" the boy said, astonished.

Then Mackie got up swiftly and, picking the bomb off the ground, hefted it to his shoulder, arched his back, and, with one limber swing, pitched it over the cliff into the sea.

Everyone swallowed, hard. But there was only the crash of waves, the withdrawing of the tide. Nothing happened. The bomb pitched impotently in the frothing current as it was drawn out to sea.

Mackie said to Junior: "Faddeh mek we gift, it return; unopen."

"— But how did you *know*?" Junior asked.

Mackie smiled and put his hand on his son's shoulder. "There is only life," he said.

IN HONOR OF DAVID ANDERSON BROOKS, MY FATHER
July 30, 1883 - November 21, 1959
A dryness is upon the house
My father loved and tended.
Beyond his firm and sculptured door.
His light and lease have ended.

He walks the valleys, now—replies
To sun and wind forever.
No more the cramping chamber's chill,
No more the hindering fever.

Now out upon the wide clean air
My father's soul revives,
All innocent of self-interest
And the fear that strikes and strives,

He who was Goodness, Gentleness,
And Dignity is free,
Translates to public Love
Old private charity.
  — *GWENDOLYN BROOKS*

GLORY

In Africa
In Africa
Some put ashes on their legs
Some held ashes in their hands
Squeezing and pressing them
into shapes

Some talked
Some silent
All deeply descended
into the ashes
—ROSS LEWALLEN

From dust to ash, from ash to dust, in Africa, America, or the West Indies, it is the same. And whether it is white shirts, black derbies, white gloves, arm ribbons of black and silver, or shiny black shoes keeping perfect time with the music, there is always the funeral, the glory road. A Southern writer once remarked that African-Americans prepare for dying all their lives. But isn't this a sensible thing to do? In the words of one African-American: "Moses died, Elijah died. All the strong men die and all the weak men die. There is no two ways about it, we all must die. So why not be ready for it, brother?"

The last century's so-called love for "buryin's," or funerals, does not say that the act of death is a moment of joy, but that the passing of the spirit is yet another celebration of life. And, as in Africa, the more important the person, the more elaborate the celebra-

The Camp Meeting. From the Collections of the Library of Congress.

tion. "I'm sure looking forward to my wake," a New Orleans woman remarked. "It will go on four nights and I'm going to have the biggest funeral the church ever had. I want a pink casket and I'm going to be wearing a pink evening dress with pink satin shoes on my feet and a pink hat on my head, so they won't look too hard at my wig."

Zora Neale Hurston, attending a funeral in Jamaica, had this to say:

> *The corpse might have been an African monarch on safari, the way he came borne in his hammock. . . . Fresh shoulders eagerly took up and all voices agreed on one song. Then there was a jumbled motion that finally straightened out into some sort of marching order with singing. Harmony rained down on sea and shore. The mountains of St. Thomas heaved up in the moonlessness; the smoking flambeaux splashed the walking herd; bare feet trod the road in soundless rhythm and the dead man rode like Pharaoh—his rags and his wretchedness gilded in glory.*

Hurston's conclusion, after attending the Jamaican wake, was that the ceremony came from the firm old African belief in "survival after death." Recently, a Rastafarian from Trinidad put it this way: "There *is* no death; there is only life." Neverthess, the famous blues-gospel guitarist-preacher Reverend Gary Davis sang it out thus: "Death don't take no holiday in this land / He come to your house / He don't stay long / Look in your bed / Somebody will be gone." Or, as the old Jamaican patriarch smoking Jackass tobacco on his porch said: "One day you see a man walking the road, the next day you come to his yard and find him dead." But this is not as lamentable as it is commendable, since the African dead are believed not just to have *lived*, but to *live*. And to *live on*. Perhaps interminably. Thus, as Hurston witnessed in the Caribbean, "the hidden roads of harmony . . . the night song had begun." There is a feeling of the commonplace in the naturalness of death—not to say a devaluation of life, but an utter acceptance of the change that takes place after one dies. The protagonist of Amos Tutuola's classic African novel *The Palm-Wine Drinkard* pays a visit to Death, and they exchange words of such mundane inconsequence that the reader forgets Death is a killer of people:

> He [Death] asked me where did I come? I replied that I came *from a certain town which was not so far from his place. Then he asked me what did I come to do? I told him that I had been hearing about him in my town and all over the world and I thought within myself that one day I should come and visit or know him personally.*

It is only afterward, in the wake of such chitchat, that the hero of the story spies the vast woodpile of Death's domain: "I saw that he was using skeleton bones of human-beings as fuel woods and skull heads of human-beings as his basins, plates, and tumblers."

There is, along with acceptance of death, a simple exaltation in life. So it was not unnatural in Haiti, a generation ago, to find the corpse of a recently dead person sitting upright in a chair with a cigarette in one hand and a rum glass in the other. To converse with the dead, even to party with same, prior to burial, is a correct African practice. For life is not just for the living. Neither is death reserved only for the dead. As the preacher said over the open cas-

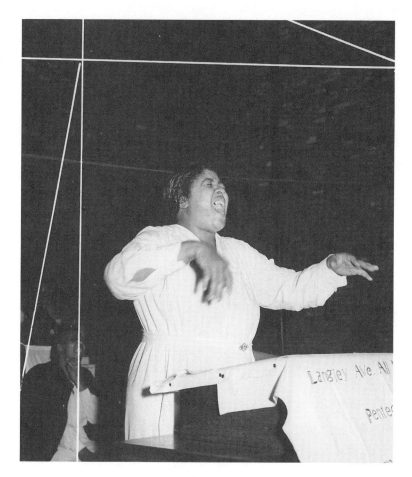

Song of Glory, Jane Tillman, Black preacher. From the Collections of the Library of Congress.

ket: "I can see the Angel Gabriel looking through the periscope of glory down the long road of time . . . he sees the weary traveler." The voices of the congregation echo:

"Nice!"

"Feels good."

"Tell it to me."

And so the conversation between the living and the dead, the quick and the still, the loud and the silent goes on, ad infinitum. The logic is in the mouths of the other parishioners:

"Mother don't want to come back to this world. Sleep on, Mother!"

"Amen, sister!"

And the voice that says all for all—"Lord, You know our names and numbers. Call us, if You please, to Glory!"

THE GLORY TRUMPETER
Old Eddie's face, wrinkled with river lights,
Looked like a Mississippi man's. The eyes,
Derisive and avuncular at once,
Swivelling, fixed me. They'd seen
Too many wakes, too many cathouse nights.
The bony, idle fingers on the valves
Of his knee-cradled horn could tear
Through "Georgia on My Mind" or "Jesus Saves"
With the same fury of indifference
If what propelled such frenzy was despair.

Now, as the eyes sealed in the ashen flesh,
And Eddie, like a deacon at his prayer,
Rose, tilting the bright horn, I saw a flash
Of gulls and pigeons from the dunes of coal
Near my grandmother's barracks on the wharves,
I saw the sallow faces of those men
Who sighed as if they spoke into their graves
About the Negro in America. That was when
The Sunday comics, sprawled out on her floor,
Sent from the States, had a particular odour;
Dry smell of money mingled with man's sweat.

And yet, if Eddie's features held our fate,
Secure in childhood I did not know then
A jesus-ragtime or gut-bucket blues
To the bowed heads of lean, compliant men
Back from the States in their funereal serge,
Black, rusty homburgs and limp waiters' ties,
Slow, honey accents and lard-coloured eyes,

Was Joshua's ram's horn wailing for the Jews
Of patient bitterness or bitter siege.

Now it was that, as Eddie turned his back
On our young crowd out fêting, swilling liquor,
And blew, eyes closed, one foot up, out to sea,
His horn aimed at those cities of the Gulf,
Mobile and Galveston, and sweetly meted
Their horn of plenty through his bitter cup,
In lonely exaltation blaming me
For all whom race and exile have defeated,
For my own uncle in America,
That living there I never could look up.

—FROM COLLECTED POEMS: 1948–1984, BY DEREK WALCOTT

GOURD

The African canteen, or drinking gourd, has as many names as uses, and it is variously called gour, gowdy, gordie, and calabash. Primarily, it is a symbol of freedom. Today, in many parts of the Caribbean, gourds remain as reminders of Africa, of gathering water by the river; of the communal ritual of water sharing. Legends are scratched in the gourd's lizardlike hide, lyrical and circular evocations of the magic tales of old.

A West Indian man was once asked what a common tree gourd was good for, and he responded with the following uses: for storing water; for decoration; for eating; for medicine. The latter, harking back to the days of slavery and the runaway Maroons, was made from the pulp of the gourd, which was mixed with kerosene oil. "It can pull out pizen," the man said, "best thing for a bullet wound."

This calls to mind the famous slave song "Foller the Drinkin' Gou'd." It was natural that the water container, which held rejuvenative power, should also be seen in the sky and be recognized as the Big Dipper. When all else failed on the Underground Railroad, the folk technique of finding Polaris, the North Star, was employed. First, it was necessary to catch sight of the Big Dipper. Then, an imaginary line was drawn through the two end stars, the so-called pointers of the Big Dipper bowl. Finally, that line was extended five times the distance between the pointers; thus was the North Star found. And so the words Drinking Gourd, Big Dipper, North Star, and Freedom were all synonymous. The great song celebrating the event of sighting in the stars the road that was the pathway to freedom goes like this:

When the sun come back,
When the first quail call,
Then the time is come;
follow the drinking gourd.

(Chorus)

Follow the drinking gourd;
follow the drinking gourd
For the old man say,
"Follow the drinking gourd."

The river's bank is a very good road,
The dead trees show the way.
Left foot, peg foot going on;
follow the drinking gourd.

(Chorus)

The river ends between two hills,
follow the drinking gourd;
another river on the other side
follow the drinking gourd.

(Chorus)

Where the little river
meets the great one,
the old man waits —
follow the drinking gourd.

According to one historian, slave legend points to the fact that

Carved Gourd by Penley. Courtesy of Lisa Remeny, Tropic Arts, Coconut Grove, Florida.

this song was, in fact, a living map. "Left foot, peg foot" may refer to a one-legged sailor who was known as Peg Leg Joe. Inciting slaves to run away north to Canada, he supposedly taught them this song, which told of how he would leave his mark in wet dark soil; first the natural foot, then the punch-hole of the peg. So goes the legend. However, regardless of the peg-leg conductor on the Underground Railroad, there is no doubt of the symbol—the gourd, the water, the North Star, the libation of freedom. To be reborn by crossing water is an African myth and ceremony brought over from ancient Egypt. The Ohio River, the "great one" cited in the song, might just as well be the Nile or the River Jordan. In any case, it was the crossing that was so important, and the link that made it possible was man, himself a vessel of water, a gourd of tribal wisdom.

Haitian Water Gourds. From the Archive of Bob Wade.

HAND

It is said that no part of the body is more eloquent than the hand. It is also believed that between the hand and the brain there is a mysterious link. An African proverb (also widely used by Europeans) promises that "One hand washes the other," which refers as much to nations as hands. Thus, as the African elder said: "I judge a man by two things primarily; his feet and his hands. If the feet are in well-kept shoes and the hands are not furtive, then I gaze into the man's eyes and see what is there. But, first, I always look to the feet and the hands."

The direct link to the mind is in the hand; in ancient times, this was clearly understood, for the hand was then the most pervasive of symbols. To the Egyptians, for instance, the female was represented in mythology and cosmology of the gods as "the other hand," the queen or princess; the hand, therefore, that brings forth the heir, "the right hand to the throne."

Egyptian stone burial reliefs portray strong images of the hand as a vessel of food, a carrier of tools, for the useful benefit of the soul in the afterlife. Ancient rock paintings in parts of Africa reveal hand images within outlines, shadings, often in conjunction with stick figures and designs.

In the late 1930s, a Belgian professor, Frans Olbrechts, realized that a group of distinctive Central African wood sculptures were not the work of a tribe, but rather of one man. From the town of Buli, in eastern Zaire not far from Lake Tanganyika, came an unexpected trove of artistic expression. Here was the first anonymous master of traditional African art to be recognized and named.

He is known today as the Buli Master. His art in wood, a blend of naturalism and expressionism, which we have come to identify with African figures in general, is famous for its elongated hands. The splayed fingers are rodlike and blunt-ended, imploring and imperfect: these are the offering and asking hands of humanity. And they are, arguably, not a distortion of nature, as much as an implementation of it. Rather, the hands are wholly human, fully intentional servants of the human form made "real" by the artist.

As phrased by writer Susan Mullin Vogel, "The Buli Master subtly violated the rules of his own artistic tradition by pushing beyond the limits of accepted stylization. The hands are just a little too big and too yearningly curved for Hemba art. They draw attention to themselves in a way that betrays a lack of the required composure and restraint." And in the expressive words of African-American writer Frances E. W. Harper:

My hands were weak, but I reached them out
To feebler ones than mine
And over the shadow of my life
Stole the light of peace divine.

It is not the naked hand, but the gloved one that speaks of certain kinds of power; particularly power withheld until the striking moment. There is, for example, the gloved might of the law officer and, conversely, of the nearly lawless inflicter of blows, the boxer. That elemental figure is, essentially, gloved to kill. Muhammad Ali once said, "A fighter's only weapons are his hands. If they go, he goes. I've been using my hands for twenty-five years striking against the hardest thing on a man's body, the head."

There are, of course, other, more subtle uses of the gloved hand, the artful hand concealed. An elder deacon spoke of "the white-gloved hands . . . reaching out, holding, carrying, soothing. Standing at the back of the last pew or down front where the

ladies could keep an eye on the congregation. Ready, able to catch those 'falling out to God.' When I think of the black church—I think of those 'ladies in white'—always wearing sparkling, pristine, white gloves that seemed the exclamation point for the white dress, hose, shoes. A tradition passed down in the church from gloved hands at baptism time. Ready to catch and hold—hold you up, so God's good could find you on your feet."

At Church, All Hands Raised. From the Collections of the Library of Congress.

The practice of healing by touch of the hand can be traced back to early times; it is probably a survival of a rite performed by the priest-physicians of ancient Egypt and Babylonia. Such monarchs as Hadrian and Constantine cured by using the hands, and it was, consequently, natural that their subjects believed them capable of imparting this influence by a glance of the eye or a mere brush of the hand.

The belief and power of the healing hand is ancient and sacred.

The laying on of hands is part of a rite practiced by ancient peoples and carried to the Americas by Native American healers and African slave shamans. Thus, the evocation of "healing power of the hand of the Lord's anointed" is a practice that continues today.

That the hand is quicker than the eye is implicit in the Egyptian and African practice of designing amulets that depicted the right hand. This was to ward off the "evil eye," and to protect the self and soul from harm's way. In the words of Zora Neale Hurston:

> *He lifted his right hand. . . .*
> *He lifted his right hand*
> *and the thing come upon me.*
> *I felt it when it come.*
> *His right hand was clothed in light.*

HEART

The Egyptian god Ptah Hotep said, "When the eyes see, the ears hear and the nose breathes, they report to the heart. It is the heart that brings forth every issue, and the tongue that repeats the thoughts of the heart." Therefore, it was from the heart of Ptah that the world was given life; and it was his words that made it so. As it was in the beginning, it is today. For the past is prologue to the present.

In the West Indies it is said, "The mind cannot know what the heart cannot leap," meaning that all intelligence comes from the experience of the heart. This experience is knowing—not believing or imagining. Such intrinsic knowing is based upon feeling. But how can feeling, raw and unproven, be the basis of true knowledge?

In Africa, as in Native America, the heart's message is that all things have life, and thus can inform. The each and the all contain feeling, and if we are patient, they will offer us their knowledge.

In Egypt, the heart was the one "life-spring" organ that all deceased ancients took with them into the afterworld. Embalmed with the body, and laid in peace, with a heart scarab amulet laid atop, the heart was the "character revealer" that spoke for the deceased at the ceremony of the heart weighing. In The Book of the Dead, the heart is thus shown in a balance scale—weighed against truth. The "Eater of Hearts" waits, if the heart is shown to be speaking untruths, to claim his prize. If truthful, however, the deceased passes to the god Osiris, who sits in the great Hall of Judgment. From there, the candidate, presented as one who is "true of voice" may be admitted into the netherworld.

Billie Holiday. Photograph by Carl Van Vechten. From the Collections of the Library of Congress.

There is an old African proverb-tale that tells of the lengths to which God went to secure heart for humankind:

God called together Sun, Moon, Darkness, and Rain. When they had gathered around, God said: "It is time for me to withdraw now where Man can no longer see me. But I will send down Heart, in my place. Now, before I take leave of you, my children, I would like to ask what each of you intend to do."

Rain spoke up first, saying: "I will pour down constantly and put everything under water."

"That is wrong," said the Creator. "Man and Woman, whom I have made, cannot live under water. You had better take turns with Sun." Rain then agreed that this was, indeed, the proper thing to do. So God next asked Sun what his intentions were going to be. "I expect to shine hotly and burn everything under me," Sun answered. Once again the Creator shook his head. "Man and Woman," he explained, "cannot live under eternal light and heat; you must give Rain a chance to refresh them." At once, Sun agreed that this would be so. After this, Darkness was asked the same question the others had been given, and he replied promptly: "I expect to rule continually."

Now the Creator sighed. "Have pity on Man and Woman," he said, "for they want to see the world I have made, and all the creatures in it. You must let Moon rule, as well as yourself." And Darkness, hearing these words, swiftly agreed. It was then that God said he had lingered too long, and so saying, disappeared. Sometime after he had left, Heart appeared, crying. "Where is our father?" he asked Sun, Moon, Rain, and Darkness. Whereupon they answered: "Father is gone, we know not where."

"Oh," cried Heart, "but I long so to be with him."

Here the story ends, in yearning innocence.

But where, the mind asks, is Heart to be found?

An African American storyteller summed it up by saying: "God gave us the longing to be near him, and that longing is always with us, in the heart."

HOME

GO HOME
They stop you
and search you
you want to

go home

they tell you to stand by
while they get inside
their car
you wait as they watch
because you want to

go home

they hold you in the hope
you will run
so you wait
because you want to

go home

they have you thinking
that to
go home

is a crime
for which
sooner or later
you will do time
so you wait
on those who

go home

whenever they
want to
and who
because you are you
and they are they
make you wait
and wonder
if you will ever

go home again
— ROHAN SAVARIAU

Home Folk. Drawing by Mariah Fox.

Home is where the heart is, or where the house is, or where, as black poet Sam Cornish says, "my ground is." In the American Northeast, the ground goes cold in winter, turns hostile. And to understand the complexity of culture, we must first look at how geography, climate, and proximity (or lack of same) to one's kind affect, not only the skin, but the skin's counterpart, the soul.

In many respects, the Northeast was an alien land to the first Africans who set foot on it. The islands of the Caribbean, where the climate was tropical, seemed much like Africa to certain slave societies. There the bushes and trees, the fields and savannas, the jungles and mountains had a familiar feel; life could get on, a toehold could be made, and there was always the possibility of escape. The Deep South must have made the heart ponder and memory linger, for though the life that was lived was bitter, the song that came out of it was sweet. The swamps and woodlands, full of strange snakes, new myths, and dangerous dogs had a sense of foreboding; but none of these compared to the nastiness of a Northeastern winter, like alum on the tongue.

In the spare chill, the desperate hours between dusk and dawn, a man had to wonder why he was made a man; and a woman a woman. For what did they have to hold on to when even their own life-giving breath, which was warm within them, exited through the mouth and promptly turned to ice? In such a strange

land, life hunkered down; home was inhale and exhale, down the centuries, all the way to the present.

Sam Cornish's recollection of his early life in cold country is, as he puts it, "the common work of memory." However, it is much more than that—more, indeed, than being raised by women in the absence of men; more than being raised on chicken and God. But not more, Cornish points out, than the winter of the blood and the gestures of love that were so hard to learn in the cold. The following excerpt is from Cornish's *Generations:*

Big L. Columbia Records. Photograph by Danny Clinch.

When I start to think of myself as a child, I always begin with winters. Do any of you remember how you learned the taste of warm milk, the smell of oil on your fingers, or the look of steps covered with ice, the first time. No. This is calendar work. All that keeps with me is the silences of my childhood winters when the absence of my father kept me close to the first two women in my life. Being alone with them, my brother and I were close for two boys, and they grew the same way. It was like the four of us in the world, living through meal time and seasons.

We lived through the dying smells of September without knowing it was the end of summer, my brother and me, long trips through streets already black with cloud, our feet loud in those empty streets of windowed shuttered houses, looking for newspapers, or smoke from passing trains. If we encountered people, I don't remember it now. It's like everything being reduced to leaves and small streets where packages of newspapers sit on the curbs.

It was the most natural thing being without a father. You just never saw him in the house. Suddenly you were in the world. No memories except you were moving around doing things. This is how it begins. It's like you were always there, and he never was.

I suppose there is a sadness to this: images of women alone in their rooms unable to drink or dance life into their long and vacant lives without husbands or relations, winters so cold the oil freezes under you, and most of all the rats that squeak in the night, the mice that walk through the kitchen looking for food, as you must have looked for food, and candies. But you lived and while you are alive there is the joy of living, this is what keeps.

I think this is what I want to write about: the life behind the broken faces or finished hands. Something goes on, even death picks the life out of your legs. I have seen it. The streets where men dig in the dust of their pockets to fool themselves. A man unable to kill because we are brothers and his knife is at your throat, and must be at his also. Hunger so deep your eyes cannot attend to the things before them. Winters so cold that the fingers break off and the hand hangs there.

But through it all we live, and it is all we will ever know.

My mother always said that we would grow up and leave her. She spent so much time saying this that my grandmother began to repeat her remark while scrubbing my back. This is the reason why to this day my back is lighter than my chest.

My grandmother was a yellow woman looking more like a visiting white lady from the big house than one of us, and at that time she almost acted like it. She was big on manners, and hard on those who picked their noses, didn't wipe after leaving the toilet; most of all she was saying that the devil would get you if you fucked around too much.

Being raised by two women who thought they were going to be left behind when the men in the family grew up, growing among two aging women who regretted their marriages was the background that made and separated my brother and me. When I want to remember him, it is always a matter of starting with the words or images of the women who, after our father's death, raised us. These women raised us on two things: chicken and God.

I knew little of the world outside, but sensed a kind of beauty in the streets that threw leaves and shadows so carefully through our house. We went to school, church, and to the house of our only relationship without being aware of the people in the street being rich, poor, middle class, or white. The only recollection we have of poverty was the day we came home and there was nothing to eat for lunch, and my grandmother made gravy from flour and water. We went back to school ready to read our books with a warm and friendly belly. This was the way I remembered it. I'm certain this was the way it was.

But this is the common work of memory. Now when I want to know myself, there is nothing for me to work with.

I start with pictures.

The street was always outside of the house. It never went any-where except under the snow. There it rested with a deeper silence than sleep. Men emerged out of the weather with red faces concealed by ice and woolen scarves. The feet itched in the boots until the snow went away. But this is a slow thing, of silence emerging black under the ice, or the crust of the snow broken by foot and shovel. The street was there after all. But it seemed to go away for awhile.

During this time of the year we were cold. All of the doors of the house remained shut, and we slept four in a bed. The single light in the house: oil lamp light after dark with the shades drawn, going over the rim, the dim flame glows behind the globe. All day she rubs the globe with newspapers and at night this clears the lamp for lighting. Outside there is the whiteness of snow and silence. I don't remember if we ate much during our winters; there was one Christmas tree that died in our house, and one turkey dinner. But winter means white curtains, the early lighting of the lamp. Up and down the streets the lights go on and off, the street car rings its bell till morning. We sleep.

I feel I have lived my life in winters. I feel my life has been the life of four people in a house surrounded by the silences of snow, the coming and going of lights in my neighbor's house. I know people lived on my street, but I never knew the color of their skin. We lived alone and in each other. Snow turns my fingers red. Snow is the color of my grandmother's dying hair. The images of winter are the ice in her dead eyes. Ice is how my growing mother slips on the winter ground. Cold is the house we live in. Our bodies the places where we stay and are warm in our home. But I ask myself if we always lived in February or December how come we were never able to speak the word love. Too busy with the blood that stands up in the skin in winter to speak of things, we can only go on living.

My mother always said we would go on without her. What else was there for us to do. Nobody stayed in these old houses; in the dark silence of those places you could only die. There my father died and my grandmother slowly rotted. Across the alley from our first home my mother sits today waiting to die. She picks among her life for things to do, as you and I, but I think she waits. Now she is older. Her children gone.

There should be no pity for her. I see in the eyes of my friends a concern, because she is a woman in an old house. Her children

thinking of children of their own, a home to finish their lives in;
what is there for her to do but sit out the seasons in dated clothing.
But I have seen her drinking at my wedding or shaking her head
when dandruff falls on my shoulders; I saw her laughing with two
teeth going brown in her mouth, and I felt her lips struggle on my
face because after thirty-one years, her sons are learning the gestures
of loving. In her small rooms in silence she sits, and she lives.

INDIGO

My blue body
moved down into the clay
holding tanks to my waist
splinters from wooden paddles
stirring distilled liquid
slowly soaked and slowly extracted
from the indigo plant
shades of blue

My blue feet
moved side by side
dried and cut blocks of solid
material/scooped from the tanks
dried in the mother sun/shades of
tiring miles walked each day/shack
to tanks to vats to field to vats
again/moving me to cotton fields
when the indigo value drops
shades of blue

My blue hands
moved between yard long vats
up to my elbows/wringing
yards of blue cotton cloth
boiling/hands ever hot and never
brown again/spreading cloth
upon the dusty, hot
ground of South Carolina/acres
of blue banners sending messages
shades of blue

                                        no blues
                        shades of crimson and gold
                                    soars
        and
                        reaches
        and
                        moved my hands/no more heat
                        moved my feet from fields
                        moved my body out of liquid
            My blue soul
—TERRI LYNNE SINGLETON

The women of West Africa say that everything that grows has color in it. God made it that way, they explain; we are not able to do it ourselves. In the case of indigo, however, there is a universal source of color, and the Yoruba of southwest Nigeria have been using it, in harmony with the deity, for centuries.

Indigo *(Lonchocarpus cyanescens)*, grows wild in Yoruba country, where it is called *elu*. It is the young leaves that are plucked, pounded with mortar and pestle, and rolled into balls. These are later dried in the sun, and an alkaline ash water is made by the women. Nothing about the process, as Terri Singleton's poem points out, is simple. All of it, from start to finish, is tedious and time-consuming, and yet the color, an oxidized blue pigment called indigo, is cherished in Africa, as well as in Europe and North America.

In Yoruba culture, every activity in life is inseparable from its religious matrix. Naturally, indigo dyeing is no different; it is closely linked with the worship of the goddess Iya Mapo, the protective deity whose eye beholds all the womanly activities of dyeing, potterymaking, oil pressing, and soap making. The origins of indigo, therefore, are attributed to myth; thus the dyer finds herself bonded to the deity in the preparation, and even exaltation, of her work.

The oldest of all blue dyes is woad, obtained from fermenting the leaves of the plant *Isatis tinctoria*. The ancient Britons painted woad on themselves in lieu of clothing, and throughout the Middle Ages woad was the most important dyestuff in Europe. Its importance, however, diminished as indigo took hold and after it was learned that indigo was a stronger dye than woad. Although the dye guilds in England and Holland tried to block passage of indigo from India, calling it the "Devil's dye," and saying it would devour anything on which it was used, indigo could not be stopped. What they have in common—woad and indigo—is the colorfast substance indigotin, which, for some reason, is present in greater concentration in indigo.

Interestingly, the demand for indigo brought about an equal

Haitian Woman. Courtesy of The American Center of Haitian Art, Matlacha, Florida. Photograph by R. D. Johnson.

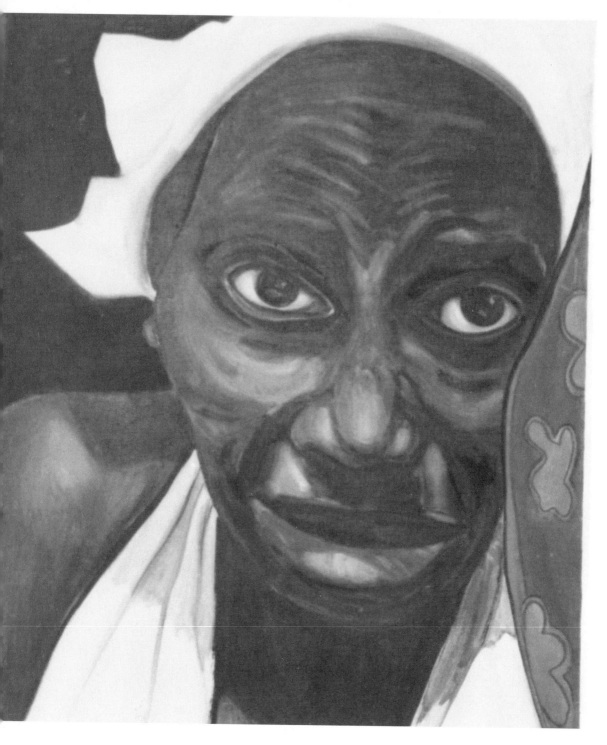

demand, in certain parts of Africa and America, for slave labor to harvest, extract, and produce it as a dye. Cotton and indigo plantations, often owned by wealthy merchants and members of the aristocracy, were established throughout the Caliphate of Nigeria. The dye, originating in Africa and thence traveling to Antigua and finally to South Carolina, was cultivated there in the mid-eighteenth century. Eventually, it became South Carolina's most profitable export; the trade peaked with a shipment of over two million pounds in 1773. So, once again, it fostered a slave society on whom the tattoo of indigo blue would stain hands and feet for generations. Ironically, the plant that birthed "Devil's dye" was used in Africa to ward off the evil eye. But whether worshiped or worn, the spirit of indigo is deeper than the vats of vanity churned out in colonial America by workers, who, waist deep in midnight blue, beat the liquid with paddles. Indigo, to many African Americans, is the robe of honor worn on the inside of the skin, the great gift of Iya Mapo.

JIVE

WE REAL COOL
The Pool Players.
Seven at the Golden Shovel.

We real cool. We
Left school. We

Lurk late. We
Strike straight. We

Sing sin. We
Thin gin. We

Jazz June. We
Die soon.
—GWENDOLYN BROOKS

Clarinet Player. Drawing by Brian Byrd, Kansas City Art Institute.

It was originally believed ("hoped" is a more accurate word) that slaves lost all trace of their original African languages when they came to the New World. Such a thought is surprising, given today's anthropological evidence. However, until the last thirty years, the historical role of black speech and its influence upon American vernacular were greatly underestimated.

According to African-American scholar Lorenzo D. Turner, "African survivals in the Gullah language of isolated black communities on the South Carolina coast" are considerable. Gullah, a form of creolized English, has a complex grammatical structure drawn from West African syntax. Patois, which is a kind of fish tea, island born and bred, also came from the west coast of Africa, and, beginning, in the seventeenth century, incorporated many European languages into its African root base. Jamaican patois, for instance, includes a spice shelf of words from English, French, and Spanish, as well as African. Papiamento, a Netherlands Antilles dialect, is a complex stew of more than half a dozen European languages into which a liberal dosage of Amerindian has also been introduced.

Slaves who were brought to the Americas from West Africa already had a knowledge of many local languages. Senegambia, the nearest part of the African coast to North America, was a major slave source for the English colonies. Slaves from that region, therefore, spoke two main languages: Wolof and Mandingo. These African languages, along with many others, contributed new words for new foodstuffs—"banana" and "yam," for instance, to name just two.

As words were added to American English from African sources, usages changed and a general "limbering" of speech patterns occurred; David Dalby, reader in West African languages at the British School of Oriental and African Studies in London, believes some of these are traceable to Senegambian influence. There is, he explains, a palpable similarity between the black American jive word "dig" and the Wolof verb "dega," which means "to understand." Dalby further states: "Several terms popularized during the jazz era also resemble Wolof. Jive in black American English means 'misleading talk,' and it can be compared to the Wolof 'jev,' meaning 'to talk disparagingly.' " A more popular use-age, however, can be "musical talk," as well.

The words "hep," "hip," and "hippie" may stem, Dalby suggests, from the Wolof verb *"hipi,"* which means "to open one's eyes." The American fifties usage of the expression "hep cat," which turned "hip" in the sixties, Dalby compares to the Wolof *"hipi-kat,"* which is, "a person who has opened his eyes." Jack Kerouac, a borrower of black talk in literature, wrote his last book in the hip lingo of a limbo-lost youth. He had already celebrated black bop talk and jazz hipsterism in *The Subterraneans,* which involves his love affair with the African American Mardou Fox, and also in his most famous work, *On the Road.* As a Canuck (as he himself put it), Kerouac was drawn to darkness—not to dark color alone, but also to the cultural milieu of night places:

Then here came a gang of young bop musicians carrying their instruments out of cars. They piled right into a saloon and we followed them. They set themselves up and started blowing. There we were! The leader was a slender, drooping, curly-haired, pursy-mouthed tenorman, thin of shoulder, draped loose in a sports shirt, cool in the warm night, self-indulgence written in his eyes, who picked up his horn and frowned in it and blew cool and complex and was dainty stamping his foot to catch ideas, and ducked to miss others—and said, "Blow," very quietly when the other boys took solos.

The gift of lyric sax translated well into Kerouac's mixed-blood prose. Moreover, he opened a whole generation to the possibilities of black-and-white artistic exchange.

The languor of cool, the rhythm of jive live on in the language of rap, which is, of course, popular with the white and black youth of today. The lexicon of cool—as a purely black phenomenon—can also be traced, some say, to West African culture. Robert Farris Thompson says: "Coolness has to do with *transcendental balance.*" In language, as in life, coolness goes back to what Thompson calls "composure under fire." This was, in fact, what drew Kerouac out of the white suburbs into the black world of detached bohemianism. "The telling point," Thompson underscores, "is that the 'mask' of coolness is worn not only in time of stress but also of pleasure, in fields of expressive performance and the dance." The interweaving of serious and comic, the yin-yang of these familiar elements, is also expressed in the Ziggy Marley song "Head Top": In almost formal lyric persuasion, Marley exalts

Background: Pharoah Sanders.
Photograph by Barbara Baumann.

spinning on the head in a popular dance rhythm which, he confides, is "an African ting."

In all of these idioms of speech and dance, it is the turning—by turns—of the hot-cold heart that gives life and language their potential to surprise. Self-control and expressive outward behavior are both learned, not innate, cultural patterns.

In the antiquity of coolness, we are taught ways of being that are thousands of years old. "Cool mouth" in Yoruba is "*enun tutu*"; in Kikuyu, "cool tongue" is "*kanua kahoro*." Both these expressions reflect intelligent deliberation, a conscious withholding of verbal play, rather than a spewing of elemental jive. This mask of the mind, this thoughtful repose, is as African as the figural sculptures that present a black mirror of reserve. However, out of this coolness may come the most consummate unfurling of sudden energy. Any moment, as Kerouac perceived in his young tenorman, the lid could blow. Here, then, is the ultimate African-Oriental medicine for our troubled world: Be bright, be calm, be cool.

Sax Tenorman. Drawing by Brian Byrd, Kansas City Art Institute.

JONKONNU

The word "Jonkonnu" has its origin in the language of the Ewe people of Eastern Ghana and Togo, whose word for deadly sorcerer is *"dzonkonu."* Today's West Indian Christmas revel and masquerade dance springs from the old African secret societies that practiced sorcery. To the present day, children are frightened at Christmastime by the appearance of Cowhead; Horsehead; the Veiled King and Queen; the Red Indian robed in feathers and replete with mirrors; the pitchy-patchy Devil whose ragged tattery dance is a-tremble with evil. Along with these ominous characters, who combine a touch of the Sorcerer's Apprentice with the decadent days of cruel slavery, there are also musicians, drummers, and fifers, who send out an equally raggledy-taggledy message.

What is this message?

It is a combination of satire and secrecy, Creole and European masquerade.

In the late eighteenth century in the islands of the Caribbean, Europeans celebrated seasonally with mummery, music, Morris dancing, polkas, and reels. Into these elaborate orchestrations befitting the high, mad monotony of the plantation era, the slaves turned their own reflection on their masters. What came out, then, was a kind of Christmas carnival, all jumbled up: Here was the polite formality of European celebration mixed in with the African antic of imitation. The dances emerged in staid beauty that frothed with sexual rivalry; they were a frontal attack on the institution of slavery and the obscure and starchy ways of the dancers' oppressors. And yet—for a time, anyway—this went unnoticed and undetected by the very ones whose hearts were set up for the satiric barbs. So the revelers had their day; but eventually their wild animism was suppressed, and, on some islands, outlawed.

The church had a hand in this, of course, feeling that the dances were decidedly pagan; and then, in 1841 the mayor of Kingston, Jamaica, banned the Jonkonnu parade, causing the famous "John Canoe Riots." However, the censors of society usually don't succeed for long, and Jonkonnu soon took to the streets again. Ernie Hinds, whose father was a Jonkonnu dancer in Jamaica, recently described the power of the troupe in his village of Oracabessa:

Gombey Drummer, Bermuda. Photograph by Barbara Baumann.

My father was the Bull in the group and his presence, large and strong and just like that animal in real life, hardly had to be masked. And yet, when he put on his costume, horned, helmeted head and ribboned, skirted pants, he was no longer just a man, but truly a great and powerful bull. I followed him one Christmas from the hills of Oracabessa where we lived to the hot sunlit streets of Ocho Rios, a distance of about ten miles. That is a long way to walk for a little boy who was given no bread or drink by his father along the way. It was a long dreary trek, rewarded at the end by the convulsive dancing and music-making in Ochi. But I will never forget that my father, the Bull, was no longer a man when he put on that mask, nor that he ignored me, his son, all the way to town and all the way back to our little village.

The following story, inspired by Ernie's all-day vigil, expresses the secrecy, the charm, the confusion and alarm that are set in motion when the time for Jonkonnu revelry is at hand. It is a kind

Gombey Drummer and Child Dancer. Photographs by Barbara Baumann.

of misbegotten fruitcake, a pageant of ancient ways that mocks and menaces, and then backs off with a doff and don of the fallen top hat and the withered crown. Jonkonnu was born of secrecy and beauty, but turned, in slave times, to parody. Today, all of these mannerisms, both sincere and affected, are present in the dancing and jigging, the drumming and singing. The following Jonkonnu tale comes from the hills of St. Mary in Jamaica. It illustrates the beauty, the poetry, and the mystery of the pageant.

One fine night when the moon was full, a duppy came to the animal people's backyard, and scared them. Now, this duppy had the head of a goat, the body of a bull, and the feet of a cat. It had a tongue of fire that licked out of its mouth, and its eyes lit up like lanterns, and smoke came out of its nose and ears.

The first person to see the duppy was Brother Mosquito, who got so scared that he ran straight into Brother Rat, who ran off, and bucked up into Brother Rabbit, who was so frightened he jumped into the air and scared Brother Monkey, who climbed all the way to the top of Anansi's palm tree, and woke him up.

"Now tell me what's so important," Anansi said, swinging down on his magic rope, "that you couldn't wait 'til morning to tell me about."

Brother Monkey's teeth were clicking and clacking, his lips were smacking, and his eyes were blinking; but he managed, somehow, to tell Anansi what Brother Rabbit had heard that Brother Mosquito had seen—a terrible duppy come to frighten the animal people.

"So," Anansi said wisely, coiling up his magic rope and sitting comfortably on a croton leaf, "Did you see the duppy with your own eyes?"

"Well," Brother Monkey admitted, "I didn't really get to see it myself; but Brother Rat almost did."

"I see," said Anansi, grinning, "and what did Brother Rat say that the duppy looked like?"

"He said that Mosquito said that the duppy was half goat and half bull and half cat," Brother Monkey said breathlessly.

"That's too many halves." Anansi laughed. "It takes just two halves to make a whole; sounds like you've got a whole and a half . . . by the way, do you remember what day it is . . . ?"

Brother Monkey looked puzzled. "What does that have to do with anything?"

"Everything," Anansi smiled. Then he told Brother Monkey to gather all of the animal people around the trunk of the palm tree, which Brother Monkey did right away.

Now, when all the animals were together, Anansi spoke to them in his finest speaking voice. "I can see that you are bothered, and perhaps more than a little frightened by Brother Mosquito's meeting tonight with a fire-breathing duppy. However, let me ask you how well you think Brother Mosquito can see?"

Now Brother Monkey looked at Brother Rat, who looked at Brother Rabbit, who looked at Brother Mosquito, who looked away, because as everyone knows, Brother Mosquito can hardly see at all. The only way he gets anywhere, which is just about everywhere, is by using his amazing sense of smell and his incredibly long nose. "Well, that just about takes care of that," Anansi chuckled, swinging out into the palmy, balmy moonlit air. "But," he added, in mid-swing, "there's one more thing I'd like to know. Does anyone know what day it is?"

The animal people looked at each other with empty looks. No one seemed to know, which was not surprising when you consider that the weather is mostly the same in the fair isles of the West Indies. But as he swung back on his magic rope, Anansi told his brothers and sisters what day, or rather what night, it was. "Why, this is the night before Christmas," he said, as he whistled through the moony air, "and that means that Brother Mosquito *did* see something that looked like a goat, a bull and cat, all mixed up for good measure— and, good reason."

Suddenly, the animal people knew what he was talking about: the Jonkonnu Dancers. "Don't you see," Anansi asked, "Brother Goat was dancing with Sister Cat and Brother Bull.

"They were wearing their scary costumes for tomorrow's Christmas parade—and that's what Brother Mosquito thought was a terrifying duppy!"

Now, the animal people looked at one another, and they saw the light of Anansi's wisdom and they heard the weight of his words.

"I don't know about the rest of you, but I, for one, feel pretty silly," Rabbit said apologetically. The others nodded knowingly, all, that is, but Brother Mosquito, who said in his whiny little voice that got on everybody's nerves: "You think you have all the answers, Anansi, but you still haven't explained the fact that the duppy breathed fire."

"Oh, that." Anansi shrugged. "There again, you only thought *you* saw a tongue of fire. Actually, what you did see, was Brother Blinky and all of his peeny-wally firefly friends!"

This time, Brother Mosquito felt the fool, up and down, and all over, and even inside out. "Well, I guess you do have all the answers," he said gloomily, for he hated to be proven wrong.

"It sure is lucky for us that Anansi puts up with all of our fool-fool ways," Brother Monkey said, and the other animal people agreed.

"Well, if I were you, I wouldn't lose any sleep over it. Besides, tomorrow is Christmas day; time to forget your cares, put away your sorrows, and think of someone other than yourself."

So the animal people thanked Anansi, and went off through the bush to their backyards and their beds, and that was the last time anyone ever saw a fire-breathing duppy until the night before Christmas the following year, when Brother Mosquito got so scared that he ran straight into Brother Rat, who ran off and bucked up against Brother Rabbit, who was so frightened he jumped into the air and scared Brother Monkey, who climbed all the way up to the top of Anansi's palm tree and woke him up.

And if this is not a true story, let the keeper of heaven's door say so now.

JUBA

Hand-clapping is one of the oldest of African musical forms, and while it may be said to share European musical elements, its practice, known as "patting juba," is wholly African. Raised to a level of self-contained accompaniment, juba—the term may have come from the word "jubilee," or *"jibba,"* for giblets—is mainly a clapping, drumming, rhythmic enterprise. However, George Washington Cable witnessed African slaves doing a juba dance in New Orleans' Congo Square long before emancipation; today, juba dance still exists on certain West Indian islands. Generally, though, the dance appears to have diminished, while juba clapping itself has never gone out of fashion. Juba rhyme, such as "Juba this and juba that / Juba killed a yellow cat," has, of course, a resemblance to rap rhythms of today. It accomplishes with tongue and toe a clackety beat, which was, during slave times, forbidden on the skin drum.

The hand was innocent, the hand was clean, and the hand could do a very spirited dance all its own—and so it did, jiving and jumping and meeting its partner head—or, shall we say, palm—on.

By the 1830s serious attention was being paid to juba's rhythmic patterns, not by musicians, but by poets who were fascinated by its metrical complexities. On December 5, 1835, Beverly Tucker wrote to Edgar Allan Poe:

I do not know to what to liken those occasional departures from regular metre which are so fascinating. They are more to my ear like that marvelous performance—"clapping Juba," than anything else. The beat is capriciously irregular; there is no attempt to keep time to all the notes, but then it comes so pat & so distinct that the cadence is never lost. . . . Such irregularities are like rests and grace notes. They must be so managed as neither to hasten or retard the beat. The time of the bar must be the same, no matter how many notes are in it.

Another of Poe's friends, Thomas Holley Chivers, was also taken with "a Jig which must be accompanied by a measured clapping of the thighs and alternately on each other. . . . There is no such rhythm as this in the Greek Poetry—nor, in fact, in any other Nation under the sun. There is no dance in the world like that of Juba—the name of that provoking jig . . . the very climax of jocularity." And Sidney Lanier, in discussing the function of pauses in poetry, found juba a potent example:

I have heard a Southern plantation "hand," in "patting Juba" for a comrade to dance by, venture upon quite complex successions of rhythm, not hesitating to syncopate, to change the rhythmic accent for a moment, or to indulge in other highly-specialized variations of the current rhythms. Here music . . . is in its rudest form, consisting of rhythm alone; for the patting is done with hands and feet, and of course no change of pitch or of tone-color is possible.

Patting juba seemed to go with persimmon beer and banjo tunes when the clap-floor rang with thumping heels, and the palms of hands danced a jig all their own: "Juber up and juber down, juber all around the town." The *codes noirs* of the West Indies, which outlawed drumming after dark, could not suppress the simple joy of the hand-clap. Nor could Georgia's pre–Civil War legal codes enforce a ban on the acculturated rhythms of hands and hands alone. Down went the drums; up went the

Background: Hand Talk. Photograph by Bobbe Besold.

hands in celebration. Patting, then, went the rounds of islands, took to the streets and hollows; and on came the other unrestrained juba-jumping instruments: the banjo, made from a gourd and a groundhog skin; the bones-turned-spoons; the triangle and tambourine.

The power of juba is, once again, a testament to the survival of blacks against all odds in the environment of repression. Bob Marley once said, "What is dark must be brought to light." What is within, therefore, must be permitted to come out. And so, with juba, what was within was spirit, life, superabundant life. No law, regardless of how harsh, could suppress the flash of hands. In Africa, the hands were man and woman, lightning and rain, sun and moon; how could these not be allowed to come and go freely, to dance of their own accord?

In the long troughs of mush and cush, the juba giblets were tossed; that is, the slaves were given leftovers, and they had to eat them to survive. Out of these troughs came the instant sustenance of liberated song—came juba. The old stuff that was left over, then, made juba; made fun, hellacious good-time free-loving fun. Out of skimpy scraps, a feast. Out of someone else's holiday—a juba, jibba, jubilee.

KEBRA NEGAST

We have read it in Revelation, Chapter Five, Verse Five: "And one of the elders saith unto me, Weep not: behold, the Lion of the tribe of Juda, the Root of David, hath prevailed to open the book, and to loose the seven seals thereof." I tell you, he loosed the seal and sent salvation to the people. The Ethiopian tradition is the Zion train home. My people, the orthodox teaching is the train, which carries no unholy.
—SHELDON CAMPBELL, LIGUANEA, JAMAICA

Ras Tafari, Emperor Haile Selassie I, Power of the Holy Trinity, Conquering Lion of the Tribe of Judah. Drawing by Mariah Fox.

The Kebra Negast is a famous, though frequently suppressed, Ethiopian classic whose title means "Glory of the Kings." The significance of this single volume, in terms of African-American and West Indian influence, is indirect, for few have read the work. However, its value is nonetheless incalculable. Over the centuries the legends, traditions, and folklore of the Kebra Negast have had an enormous worldwide effect on people of African descent. How is this possible, since the book itself is not widely read? The answer is simple: the Kebra Negast may well be the African equivalent of the Bible, and its contents are familiar—in the form of legends—to African people. In Abyssinia, for instance, it has been, and still is, venerated as containing the "final proof" of the people's descent from the Hebrew Patriarchs. The kinship of these Solomonic kings is, therefore, in direct line with Jesus Christ.

In August of 1872 Emperor John of Ethiopia wrote to Lord Granville of England: "There is a book called *Kivera Negust* which contains the Law of the whole of Ethiopia, and the names of the Chiefs and Churches and Provinces are in this book. I pray you find out who has got this book, and send it to me, for in my country my people will not obey my orders without it."

The great storehouse of myth in the Kebra Negast stems from many tributaries: the Old Testament; rabbinical texts; and Egyptian, Arabian, and Ethiopian sources. Of the book's compilation and its maker little or nothing is known, but the principal groundwork came from traditions that were current in Syria, Palestine, Arabia, and Egypt during the first four centuries of the Christian era. Speculation is that the earliest composition of the Kebra Negast was in the sixth century A.D. Its compiler was probably a Coptic priest, for the books he used were writings accepted by the Coptic church.

In succeeding centuries, as a result of widespread conquests by Islam the Coptic text was wholly or partly translated into Arabic. During that time, when the Zague kings reigned over Ethiopia and the Solomonic line was broken, the translation of the Kebra Negast into Amharic was punishable by death. So the book, though it existed in Arabic and Coptic, was not, at that time, rendered into the language of its origin. Still, the legends that were the fount of its wisdom were known and revered in spite of the sanctions that were levied against their source.

What are these legends?

One central theme in Ethiopian myth is that when God made Adam,

Koran, Northern Africa. Courtesy The Lowe Art Museum, University of Miami.

he placed a pearl in his body. It was intended that this symbol of divinity should pass from one holy person to another; the mother of Samuel, whose name was Hannah, received it; and it is written that the pearl passed through the body of Solomon and the body of Christ. And so it was that it entered Menelik, the son of Solomon by the Queen of Sheba. The lineage, therefore, spans the centuries, reappearing in a modern context, espoused by the Rastafarian faith. Haile Selassie, the late emperor of Ethiopia, it is believed, was himself a kinsman of Christ, and thus a divine being, a deity.

The idea of the divine origin of kings in Ethiopia, the Sudan, and Egypt is, indeed, quite ancient. It also parallels the myth of the succession of the pearl. Many an Egyptian king, for instance, stated that he reigned "in the egg." By this we are meant to understand that he ruled before birth; that the egg was, so to speak, as a pearl deposited in his mother by the sun god, who was his father.

As the 225th—heir to the Solomonic throne, Haile Selassie, even as a boy, confounded his detractors by having an almost unfathomable knowledge of his own lineage. It is said that he was well acquainted with arcane Coptic literature, Egyptian necromancy, cabalistic doctrine, and the ancient Abyssinian deities of earth, water, and war. When he came to Jamaica on a state visit on April 21, 1966, the long-awaited savior of African people was greeted by a hundred thousand Rastafarian and African-Jamaican believers. Calabash drums and Abeng bullhorns—unchanged since the Ashanti wars—were also there to greet this small and humble old man who, when he saw the commotion created by his visit, began to weep. According to Timothy White (author of *Catch a Fire: The Life of Bob Marley*), "The crowd cried with him, many Rastas remembering the biblical passage which said that Christ wept when he beheld the multitudes." White also mentions that many Rastas were aware that Selassie's palms "had the holy stigmata—nail prints just like those of the risen Christ."

The Rastafarian Nazarites, members of the present messianic movement, have spiritual roots that date back thousands of years.

When Haile Selassie (whose was also known as Ras Tafari Makonnen) was proclaimed emperor of Ethiopia in 1930, many Africans, as well as African Americans and West Indians, believed that a new day was at hand. Marcus Garvey, another great advocate of black liberation, had already pointed his prophetic finger toward Africa and said: "One God! One aim! One destiny!" Yet it is the King James Bible that sums it up perfectly and gives dramatic proof to people of their birthright and blessing: "Princes shall come out of Egypt; Ethiopia shall soon stretch out her hands unto God" (Psalm 68, verse 31). Today, through drought and famine and internecine war, the legend of the house of Makonnen lives on—or, as poet-prophet Bob Marley put it, "lives out," for the Rastafarian faith is deep, and it treasures the sacred blood of Solomon, and like rings in a great pool of water, it spreads out.

"I am thy father." (The deity Ptah-Tanen addressing Rameses the Great.)

KUMINA

Kumina, an ancient ancestor cult, is regarded today as one of the most "African" of all Caribbean religions. It was founded, it is believed, by free Africans, who came to the island of Jamaica in the middle to late 1800s. Noted Jamaican writer Olive Senior has written:

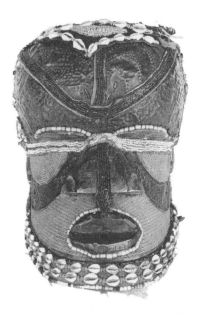

Kuba Helmet Mask from Zaire. The Lowe Art Museum, University of Miami.

Research has indicated quite clearly a Bantu, more specifically Congo, ancestry of this cult, and voluntary migrants from the Congo (now Zaire) were sent to the St. Thomas area of Jamaica. The language of the ritual has been shown to be largely Ki-Kongo. The name Kumina also seems to be of Bantu origin. Among possible sources are the following Ki-Kongo words: Kumina—to move or act rhythmically; Kumunu—a well-known traditional dance rhythm; kumu—to mount up.

Kumina worshipers, whose roots, they say, go back to the Bongo nation (of the Congo-Niger watershed area) believe that if the dead are not sent away properly on their journey to the after-world, then their spirit, or duppy, will appear as a malign influence on the living. Kumina rites of passage, therefore, are performed at the normal cultural transitions in life—birth, death, marriage, and memorial. The ceremonies are noted for the introduction of trances among its participants. This is not surprising to one who has seen, heard, and participated in Kumina proceedings.

There is nothing quite like rounding a turn on a steep Jamaican road, high in the mountains, and suddenly hearing the explosion of goatskin Kumina drums echoing out of a small peak-roofed, cliff-hanging church. The blood beat of those hollow wooden drums stays with you for hours, even days. In addition to the handmade drums, one might also hear scrapers, shakers, and catta sticks. These may be fashioned from cheese graters, hollowed-out gourds, and perhaps guava branches carved into drumsticks.

The drumming of Kumina is open to men only; the so-called cast drummers serve a long apprenticeship and are highly respected members of the Kumina group. The ceremony itself involves drumming and dancing, the latter led by the Kumina leader, a man or woman, whose psychic strength is such that he or she can control the spirits that visit the ceremonial. As in Haitian vaudou, when the spirit wishes it "mounts the horse," or person thus possessed. The spirit may be of earth, sky, or underworld; however, in today's practice only the "positive" ancestor spirits are "answered" by the dancers.

Ogoni Spirit Mask from Nigeria. The Lowe Art Museum, University of Miami.

Spirit Mask, African, Dan (Ivory Coast); 19th century, wood. The Lowe Art Museum, University of Miami.

One can only imagine what a Kumina ceremony must have been like before the turn of the century. Spirit possession, while exotic-romantic to some, is actually a frightening thing to watch; the body is a helpless host in convulsive overload, responding to an invisible daemon that, through the ceremony, must be exorcised. Some years ago, on a late night at Blue Harbour, overlooking the town of Port Maria, a drum master from Ghana showed how ghosts were liberated with drums. The beat he laid down, hand over hand, was a kind of Mama-Papa rhythm (just say the words while clapping the beat), repeated endlessly. The duppy-chasing hollow report of the coconut-log drum reverberated through the night, traveling across the water of the bay. It was heard, they said the following morning, many miles away. And that night, they also said, the duppies went elsewhere.

LION

*. . . and he turned
aside to see the
carcass of the lion:
and, behold, there
was a swarm of
bees and honey
in the carcass
of the lion.*

*And thus,
as Samson discovered,
Out of the strong,
came forth sweetness.
From the golden lion
was rendered golden honey.*
— *BY GERALD HAUSMAN & KELVIN RODRIQUES*

African myth suggests that the lion's skin is the gold of a subter-
ranean sun. In ancient Egypt, the lion presided over the annual
floods of the Nile, because the raging waters—like the roaring
lion—coincided with the entry of the sun into the zodiacal sign of
Leo during the dog days. Lion hearted, brave as a lion, hungry as a
lion . . . the risen sun a youthful lion; the setting sun an old or
infirm one. So run the myths of feline magnificence, the very
word "lion" conjuring images of sun fire and power, the strength
of manhood, the dignity of old age and honor. To kill a lion and
eat of its flesh in many African cultures was an act of greatness; a

youth's proving ground on the way to becoming a man; a man's fulfillment, at any age, of that promise in himself—to be always, in all things, brave.

Lion myths are heraldic in African, medieval European, and Native American lore. The male lion is mystically united with the sun, while the lioness is usually kin to the moon—in one Amerindian myth, she nibbles it wafer thin. The lion's presence, in any case, speaks of nobility. Even the tail is shaped like the flame-tipped point of a spear. Bushmen believe that this emblem of the lion is the means by which it can speak. If the lion so chooses, he can put his tail in his mouth and talk to human beings. The Khoikhoi, a pastoral people of South Africa, venerate the lion, but they believe that it was not always a beast of the earth. They say that the lion once lived in trees like a bird, and only came down to earth because of a sorcerer's curse.

Above and in background: Lion Monoprints. Ross LewAllen.

The lion-and-tree motif is echoed in yet another Bushman myth:

Once there was a young man who fell asleep on a hunt, and was taken by a hungry lion. To save himself, the youth pretended to be dead, whereupon the lion carried him up a tree and deposited him between some branches. Then he went away to slake his thirst. When the lion returned, the young man was gone, having returned to his village. There, his mother hid him, but the lion soon came and threatened the whole community unless the youth was turned over to him. They, in turn, fought the lion with arrows and spears, but to no avail. In the end, they threw other villagers to him. However, the lion was vehement about having the youth who had tricked him; he wanted no other.

Finally, the mother decided the fate of her son: "Be it so. Give my child to the lion. In no wise, however, must you allow the lion to eat him, in no wise must you allow the lion to continue walking about here. You must kill him and lay him upon my child. Let the lion die and lie upon my son."

According to mythologist Paul Radin, "the basic theme of this tale is that Nature can, after a fashion, misunderstand its relation to man just as man his relation to Nature." Further, it is the lion's endowment of speech that juxtaposes him with man as a celebrated equal, one who can make demands and show the bargaining power of authority. It is this, in the long run, that Africans have assimilated into their culture and that other African cultures—American and West Indian—have also incorporated into their lives: the living icon of the lion, as in the Lion of Judah.

The lion becomes the man, just as the man, in reverse, becomes the lion. The symbolism of such an exchange is evident in the mother's cautionary, ceremonial dictate: "You must kill him and lay him upon my child. Let the lion die and lie upon my son." No mention made of the youth's death, though it is clearly implied. He is, in a sense, coalesced with the spirit, the totemic power of the lion.

There is a similar African tale, childlike in its innocence, of a lion hunt told by Kamante, the hero of Isak Dinesen's *Out of Africa*:

One day another lion had to kill. It was coming from far off Masailand. . . . Mutua saw the lion hidden in a thicket. They all had guns. Then Mutua thought of going near the thicket to see how the lion entered in. By then, the lion had gone inside. He had turned head on the way, finally, so that when Mutua looked, he met face with this lion. He, Mutua, had a gun with him but he could not move. Then the lion went swop with a lot of bushes on the man. It lied on him. It tried to look for the man and the man was hidden underneath the bushes. So the other people shot it to death lying on the man and still the man couldn't move. Nobody wanted to go near it because then they thought it was not dead. By this time, there was a certain boy who had a knife. He went step by step looking that lion not wake up and kill them all. He met it dead. So Mutua was still with his gun, not harmed at all.

Lion Photograph. Ross LewAllen.

Yet another lion encounter, certainly a rite of passage, is recorded by the poet Ross LewAllen:

Kivon, the Masai who could tell time on the savanna grass blades or the shadows of a giraffe's neck, had known for years the very ground that lions love. He knew the invisible straight lines that lions walk when they stalk their prey. The lions I met in Kenya walking these lines seemed like ships on a sea of grass, their sails full, their bows pointed on a perfect bearing, the sailing simbas.

One day, Kivon announced, "Come with me."

What kind of trust walk was I on? I could only measure the distance to the lion in seconds. If it decided to charge, I couldn't have reached the vehicle, and safety. I had crossed some invisible line that the lion owned. Shivers ran up and down my back and legs. My knees weakened. Here I was with miles and miles of earth around me, the African sky above me, and I had stepped into Kivon's time with lions. This timepiece had no gears, springs, ticking, hour hand, second hand. It was made up of this parameter of African soil that the lion owned. I was guided there by Kivon, through my own fear. I met the lion then through a kind of mutual trust; and for me, it was not unlike the Masai rite of walking into the lion's roar, showing no sign of fear in the face of the lion whose "thunder," as Isak Dinesen once said, was "ready in his chest."

American pulpits have rung with the clamor of lionization in parable, song, and sermon. Daniel in the lion's den; David's bodyguard, who slew a lion; the lion-faced warriors of God; the princely tribe of Judah proclaiming a lineage of lions. We still speak metaphorically of bearding the lion and it is in the face of the Pharaoh that we may also see the lion's almond-eyed likeness and the false beard upon the shaven chin. Part falcon, part cobra, part lion, he was brother-god to those who lent him their skin and eye and facile brain. As a noble figure, he was irresistible; on the battlefield he was immortal. Moreover, as African Americans understand today, the pharaoh was black. So it is in the "blackness" of biblical imagery that the people see a welcome reflection. In the minds of contemporary African Americans lionheartedness comes not by blindly accepting a borrower's European standard, but by embracing the model from which it sprang: the lineage of the African lionhearted king. Let the lion, at last, put tail to tongue and speak like a man.

Lion of Judah. Drawing by Mariah Fox.

MERMAID

There is a story that some say is African American and others claim to be Native American; it is the story of the mermaid. The tale begins with a Catholic priest, who appeared among the peaceful Pascagoula, a Native American tribe, in Mississippi sometime around 1727. Charles Gayarre repeated the tale in 1903, pointing out that the priest's purpose was "to wean the Indians away from mermaid-worship to the religion of the Cross; the mermaid, however, presently appeared and by her singing lured the entire tribe to march, also singing, into the Bay of Biloxi, whence their voices can still sometimes be heard."

Here the legend seems to drop back into the mystery of its birth; a land of mist, moss, and mystic tales. Who can know, for instance, if the mermaid, seen by witnesses "at twelve o'clock on Christmas eve, when the moon is at the meridian," was merely a passing manatee? Who can know if the participants were really Indian? Some say they were neither Biloxi nor Pascagoula, but Ibo people, fresh from Africa, who, under the leadership of their chief, are said to have marched, singing, into Dunbar Creek on St. Simons, one of the Sea Islands off the coast of Georgia. Seminole blacks, it has been confirmed, descendants of runaway slaves from Georgia and South Carolina, certainly know the story.

One version of the mermaid myth, going back to slave times, is told by Mississippi storyteller J. D. Suggs:

Facing page: The Water Mumma, Mama Erzuli, Ezili. The American Center of Haitian Art, Matlacha, Florida; photograph by R. D. Johnson.

Before they had any steam, ships were sailing by sails, you know, across the Atlantic. The Atlantic was fifteen miles deep, and there were mermaids in those days. And if you called anybody's name on the ship, they would ax for it, "Give it to me." And if you didn't give it to them, they would capsize the ship. So the captain had to change the men's names to different objects—hatchet, ax, hammer, furniture. Whenever he wanted a man to do something, he had to call him, "Hammer, go on deck and look out." The mermaid would holler, "Give me hammer." So they threwed the hammer overboard to her, and the vessel would proceed on. The captain might say, "Ax, you go on down in the kindling room start a fire in the boiler; it's going dead." Then the mermaid says, "Give me ax." So they have to thrown her an iron ax. Next day he says, "Suit of furniture, go down in the stateroom and make up those beds." And the mermaid yells, "Give me a suit of furniture." So they had to throw a whole suit of furniture overboard.

One day he made a mistake and forgot and said, "Sam, go in the kitchen and cook supper." The mermaid right away called, "Give me Sam." They didn't have anything on the ship that was named Sam; so they had to throw Sam overboard. Soon as Sam hit the water she grabbed him. Her hair was so long she could wrap him up—he didn't even get wet. And she's swimming so fast he could catch breath under the water. When she gets home she goes in, unwraps Sam out of her hair, says: "Oooh, you sure do look nice. Do you like fish?" Sam says, "No, I won't even cook a fish." "Well, we'll get married." So they were married.

After a while Sam begin to step out with other mermaids. His girl friend became jealous of him and his wife, and they had a fight over Sam. The wife whipped her, and told her, "You can't see Sam never again." She says, "I'll get even with you." So one day Sam's girl friend asked him, didn't he want to go back to his native home. He says yes. So she grabs him, wraps him in her hair, and swum the same fastness as his wife did when she was carrying him, so he could catch breath. When she come to land she put him onto the ground, on the bank. "Now if he can't do me no good he sure won't do her none." That was Sam's experience in the mermaid's home in the bottom of the sea.

Then he told the others how nice her home was, all fixed up with the furniture and other things. There weren't any men down there— guess that's why they ain't any mermaids any more. Sam said they had purple lips, just like women are painted today. You see pictures of mermaids with lips like that. In old days people didn't wear lipstick, and I think they got the idea from seeing those pictures.

Sam told the people the mermaid's house was built like the alligator's. He digs in the bank at water level; then he goes up—nature teaches him how high to go—then digs down to water level again, and there he makes his home, in rooms ten to twenty feet long. The mermaid builds in the wall of the sea like the alligator. Sam stayed down there six years. If he hadn't got to co'ting he'd a been there yet, I guess.

Today, the Pascagoula mermaid myth can be followed from Biloxi, Mississippi, where on the banks of the bay it was told to us by native Mississippian James Clois Smith, Jr.; and from there, it threads its way to Castle Gordon, Jamaica, where the old legend is so much alive, you can actually meet a man who has seen—or believes he has seen—the fish woman herself. The mermaid, known to many people in the village, is like the Holy Grail. Some say that by meeting her a person gains some special sight, and is blessed. Others believe that once you have laid eyes on her, you become "a little touched." In any case, the tale of the encounter, retold here from a story given by Sweet Sweet, a storyteller in Castle Gordon, goes as follows:

I saw the mermaid staring at me. Her head appeared larger than the rest of her body because of the swirling of her hair.
As she moved her lips, I heard her speak.
"What are you doing here?"
"Drinking."
Her skin was the color of dark honey, and all around her head,

Background: Fishtail, North Coast, Jamaica. Watercolor by Lisa Remeny, Tropic Arts, Coconut Grove, Florida.

her gold, wiry hair rose and fell like water weeds in a secret current. I saw when she smiled that she had little gray teeth, fishlike and sharp. Around her head and hair, there fanned a school of bright minnows.

The mermaid saw me looking at the fish.

"My children," she remarked, "my babies."

I said nothing.

The children of the mermaid were whirling about her gold seaweed hair, making crescents and curves with their shiny fins.

"Tell me, man, what do you eat?"

I followed the spinning fish with my eye.

"What do I eat? Why, fish, of course."

At this, she turned tail and plunged to the bottom of the spring, her children sparkling down into the deeper water with her. I could see them, glimmering in the blue depths of the pool.

Yet another version of the same tale reaches farther back in Jamaican time to the Columbus landing near Discovery Bay. It goes as follows:

One day a shaman of the Arawak told Columbus's men that there was indeed a secret inland river in whose milky water there lived a goddess, half-woman and half-fish. She was lovely to look at, the shaman said, for her hair was longer than her tail.

When the men from the Columbus party expressed interest in seeing the mysterious fish woman with their own eyes, the shaman agreed to take them there. He did so the following day. What greeted their eyes was a woman whose hair was filled with the light of the sun. Sure enough, from the waist down she was all fish, scaly and covered with slime. But her upper body was a beautiful woman's, and her hair was the spun gold of the sun itself. For a long time the transfixed men regarded this pleasant apparition: the fish woman sitting on the riverbank, combing her bright hair with a golden comb.

Then the leader of the men spoke to the shaman. "I must have that comb," he said. The shaman shook his head. "That you cannot have," he replied. *The Spaniard at once became enraged and, throwing the shaman aside, he ran forward. Instantly, the fish woman plunged off the riverbank into the water; and the mad Spaniard went after her. At the same time, the shaman recovered himself, and he, too, jumped into the water.*

All three disappeared, never to be seen again. But they say on moonlit nights, you can hear the fish woman singing, and some people have seen her, a vision trembling on the soft current, combing her long golden hair.

The last incarnation of the myth journeys back, as it should, to its source in Africa.

Along the banks of a river near the village of Betsimisaraka in Madagascar, the mermaid appeared to a fisherman whose hook was caught in her hair. "You may marry me," she said to the fisherman as he freed her, "but you must never tell anyone what I am."

Many people in the village wondered how so poor a fisherman could have such a beautiful wife, but always he guarded her secret, which was also his own. In time, they had four children, two boys and two girls. The poor fisherman was then the happiest man there was, but one day, having drunk too much rum, he felt like boasting to his friends. Thoughtlessly, he gave his wife's secret away.

At that very moment, his beautiful wife left their home and returned to the river with her two daughters. Although the sons remained with their father, he was no longer a happy man; nor did he ever lay eyes upon the boys' mysterious mother again.

She has many names and many origins the world over, but in African myth, she, the mermaid, mumma, water mother, is the spirit, the very heart of water. In marrying a man of earth, or even merely making contact with one, she becomes a spirit both of water and of earth. In myth, these two polarities always seek to be reunited, as they once were, long ago in the beginning of time.

MOTHER

MOTHERS SING BEFORE THE RAIN

Sitting very straight on a bus, ironing-board straight back, and her daughter, just like her, beside her, the same kind of back country straightness, while all round the bouncing bus, loaded with great sacks of yams, the slack men smoke cigarettes and joke among themselves. Then, coming down from the John Crow mountains, we hear, in the river valleys, the voices of women lifted in song. They are singing under the bamboo leaves, pounding shirts and shorts on river rocks, singing. Rock, river, stone, shirt; and the song that comes from this is rain, though we haven't had any for weeks, and the rivers are almost dry. Miss Jenny tells us: "My mother sang like that and she died in my arms at the age of one-hundred-and-something, no one knows how old they are in the town of Friendship. I took care of her until she was ready to go and then I sang her to sleep the way she used to sing me to sleep when I was little, and she went like that, peacefully, smiling into my eyes as she walked away to heaven." The bus backs into the marketplace where the men are all carrying sacks like donkeys and they are butchering goats and buying goods, while the women—mothers with babies, young girls, pretty girls, pregnant girls—are sitting beside the blue sea selling cho-cho, white yam, yellow yam, potato, carrot, thyme, onion, garlic, melon, cassava, cucumber, june plum, naisberry, otaheite apple, soursop, sweetsop, julie mango, black mango, lime, pawpaw, pumpkin. Suddenly it starts to rain, a hard man's rain, and the men are moving now to the rhythm of the rain on the zinc roof of the market while the women continue as if nothing were happening, selling, marketing, tending their young, not bothering with the men who carry-come and bring and now, right now, start, for the first time, to sing.
— GERALD HAUSMAN & KELVIN RODRIQUES

Background: Mother and Child. Drawing by Teri Sanders, Kansas City Art Institute.

The mother of a newly dead child wept bitterly and her cries went up to God, who took pity on the woman and told her to bury the child in a deep marsh. A month later a plant began to grow from the spot where the child had been buried. It grew up and bore grains, which birds came to eat when they were ripe. Then God told the woman to pound the grains, cook and eat them. This was the beginning of rice, so called after the name of the child.
— MALAGASY MYTH

Migrant Worker, Potato Season.
From the Collections of the
Library of Congress.

It was said by the ancient Egyptian scribe of the palace of Nefer-tari: "Thou shalt never forget thy mother. For she carried thee long beneath her breast and after thy months were accomplished she bore thee. Three long years she carried you upon her shoulder. She nurtured thee, and took no offense from thy uncleanliness."

From "The Promised Land." Courtesy of Kitty King (OWI Collection, the Library of Congress).

The poet and reggae artist Peter Tosh speaks of his root-mother, Mama Africa: "Long time me no see you, mama; they hide you, mama, but I search and I find . . . in you there's so much beauty, in you there's so much life . . . you are the maker of coal, you are the maker of diamonds . . . you are my mother, Africa; you are my father, Africa."

The longing and love for the great mother of antiquity is replete with the worship of black motherhood. For upon her rested the continuity of the race, and as Camara Laye has written, "The mother is there to protect you. She is buried in Africa and Africa is buried in her."

Three men went before God and told Him of their needs. The first wanted a horse, the second a dog, the third requested a woman. The three departed with the things which they desired, but on the way home, a great rain came and forced them into the bush for three days.

Now the horse and the dog were not of much use in the downpour. However, the woman prepared meals for the three men, which cheered them greatly. When the rain stopped, the three returned to God and asked if they might exchange the horse and dog for two more woman. They left satisfied, but the woman who came from the horse ate all the time and the one who came from the dog was mean.

The first one, though, the original woman, was good; and it is she who is the mother of all mankind.
— *TOGO MYTH*

What is the greatest sacrifice any mother can give?

Without question, we would say, life, the life of her children. For the mother's presence is the heart's blood of life, its nurturing source, the earth that fills the void and makes possible the breath of the mortal infant.

But the greatest sacrifice, according to poet Terri Lynne Singleton, is not only in nurturing the race, but in returning it whence it sprang: the true repository of all life, Mama Africa. Singleton cites the true story of a slave woman, who escaping from North Carolina to Ohio via the Underground Railroad, found brief sanctuary in a barn. (The story is also eloquently told in a different form by Toni Morrison in her novel, *Beloved*.)

There, while she hid her children in the hay, and herself with them, she heard from the road the sound of voices, searchers coming to find them. While the owner of the house showed the men that it was empty, the slave mother crouched in fear in the nearby barn. Time passed, and finally the men left, satisfied that she wasn't there. The woman who owned the house came outside to find that the slave mother had slit both of her children's throats in the darkness of the barn.

In the diary that describes this incident, the escaped slave gave her rationale: That once on free soil, she wanted her children to remain free forever. By killing them, she gave them life; sent them back to their homeland, to the mother of all, Mama Africa. Terri Lynne Singleton writes, "The slave mother who gave her children death also gave them life, and as she escaped in the flesh, following the way North, they escaped in spirit, altogether, never to be separated again." Such a story can only be understood by one who knows—not just believes—that life is everlasting; that in life there is death; that in death there is life. The concept is not occidental, and it confounds the mind bent on absolutes. However, as stated

Background: Mother Africa. Woodcut by Carlos Aguirre.

by J. A. Rogers, "the portal through which life passes in and emerges out into the world is black."

In the words of the poet Carolyn Rogers: "My mother. . . sturdy black bridge that I crossed over on." The bridge of ages and of ashes spanning life and death, combining motherhood and fatherhood in one selfless, simple gesture: giving birth.

GONE HOME FREE
Hidden
   Still
      Moving swiftly
           Water—Fields—Hills—Swamps
                Feet as wings
                    Heart as messenger
Moving swiftly
Freedom seeking

Hidden
   Passing
      Moving swiftly
           House—Closet—Field—Barn
                Lamps as beacons
                    Strangers as saviors
Moving quietly
Freedom nearer

Hidden
   Shadows
      Moving swiftly
           Searching—Seeking—Close—Threatened
                Dogs as betrayers
                    Men as jailers
Moving steady
Freedom threatened

Hidden
   Panic
      Moving swiftly
             Knife—Prayer—Resolve—Decision
                 Voices now silenced
                       Angels not slaves
Moving home
Freedom here

Hidden
   Borders
      Moving swiftly
             Run—Hands—Warmth—Rest
                 Spirits not captives
                       Souls gone on ahead
Moving on
Freedom
Gone on home
                 Free.
—*TERRI LYNNE SINGLETON*

NAME

he old African practice of naming a child according to the day of the week on which he or she was born was common in both the Caribbean Islands and in America during the late 1700s. Certain of these names still exist on the island of Jamaica where it is certainly not uncommon to hear the Friday name, Cuffee or Kofi.

Man	Woman	Day
Cudjoe	Juba	Monday
Cubbenah	Beneba	Tuesday
Quaco	Cuba	Wednesday
Quao	Abba	Thursday
Cuffee	Pheba	Friday
Quamin	Minba	Saturday
Quashee	Quasheba	Sunday

Frederic G. Cassidy, Jamaican linguistics expert and author of *Jamaica Talk*, quotes from a 1774 text: "Quashic was already taken as a typical name for a negro," as Long indicates in another place when he describes the fate of the educated children of a white planter and a negro mother.

El The Sensai and Tame One. From Artifacts, Courtesy of Big Beat/Atlantic (photograph by Chi Modu).

He is soon, perhaps, left to herd among his black kindred, and converse with Quashee and Mingo, instead of his school fellows, Sir George, or My Lord; while mademoiselle, instead of modish French, must lean to prattle gibberish with her cousins Mimba and Chloe.

By the time Tom Cringle's Log *was published in 1834, the name Quashee, rendered Quashie, was reduced to a generic term for* peasant *and also for* fool. *Quasheba had already been denigrated, even before 1800, to "the colored mistress of a white man."*

Writing in 1851, however, J. V. Cobb made the following important distinction about four native Africans, who were slaves in Georgia. Named Capity, Saminy, Quominy, and Quor, the four "were treated with marked respect by all the other Negroes for miles and miles around." The suggestion here is obvious: The cultural value of a name is relative to the culture which embraces it.

From left to right: DJ Ralph M, Tomahawk Funk, and Sondoobie from the group "Funkdoobiest." Immortal Records/Epic.

African names, therefore, conferred a certain distinction on slaves who were permitted to keep them. In addition, many eighteenth-century slave names begin to show the influence of Native American heritage; whether a name is African or Indian, it is sometimes hard to tell: Maneta, Moosa, Monimea, Paya, Sauny, Sebany, Tremba, Yaumah, Yearie, Yonaha, Yono Cish.

It is the thesis of storyteller Benjamin Oswald Brown, whom the authors met in the parish of St. Mary in Jamaica, that most black men have three names of the following order: birth name, nickname, common name. That is, the name you are given at birth, which is formal; a name associated with childhood and growing-up time; and finally a name that is a kind of adult accretion, often symbolic of work, play, or pastime.

Brown also explains that the convenience of three names was also quite practical. "Suppose," he says, "my friend, Roy, got into some trouble, and the police came looking for him. They would use his formal name, wouldn't they? In the country, where he might disappear, no one would know him by that name; only by the name Slouchy, his second, or childhood name."

The generic fourth name, Brown continued, was merely a designation of a place or area. So that a certain fellow by the name of Vincent, who was known by the place where he lived, Bailey's Vale, was rarely called by his first name. Such names as Aberdeen, Alabama, Boston, Dallas, and Dublin were common in the slave era—some chosen by slave parents, others by masters to indicate point of purchase.

The practice of assigning casual names, place names, and adopted names may have been augmented during slave times. As N. N. Puckett remarks in *Names of American Negro Slaves:* "The slave himself may well have enjoyed playing around with the spoken word. Slaveboy Malachi, for instance, was baptized seven times, under different names, and with different sponsors, the good rector, to whom all young negroes looked alike, not recognizing him."

A casual glance at a roster of African-American names today will show the same sprinkling of homily, homespun, homeboy classification, the same style of name choosing as prevailed three hundred years ago. Snoop Doggy Dog might well be the antebellum fellow named Jump-Frog or Cooter. Comedian Redd Foxx did not hide his origin-sounding stage name; there were plenty of smart foxes and nosy hounds on the old plantation. And once again, the names of today hark back still further, reaching all the way to Africa: Mutabaruka, Cuffee, Kareem, and Kumara. The tendrils of names, the fecund roots of Africa; the geography, history, memory, and imaginations of the people, growing and changing, but always part of their ancestral past. In such a magnificence of names, we sense the listening fire, the whispering trees, the wise shadows of the lost past.

NINE NIGHT

In Nine Night, a primarily African ritual, the body as well as the spirit of the dead is cleansed, purified, and sent on its way to the spirit world. Similar to an Irish wake, the Nine Night ceremony, still common in the Caribbean today, takes place at the home of the deceased. During the first eight days, the body is prepared for burial. In the old days this meant stopping the orifices with "plugs" of coffee, sponging the body with lime, and tying the jaw shut with string. On the island of Haiti, the body is then properly dressed and put in a chair, and the wake begins. Cigarettes and white rum are customarily offered to the dead person as if he were alive. On the island of Jamaica, during the eight days prior to the ninth night and final burial, family and friends gather round, playing dominoes and board games. The ninth night is usually reserved for the dispersal of the dead person's belongings and the singing of traditional chants and songs, which lasts until dawn, when the body is finally put to rest in the earth. According to the East Indian Jamaican custom, on the ninth night after death a plate of food is placed under a large silk-cotton tree. Often called the ancestor tree, the silk cotton, which came from Africa, was and is thought to contain the spirits of departed ancestors. This final plate of food is for the duppy, the spirit of the dead, who is asked to partake of one last supper before going on his way.

In the parish of St. Mary, Jamaica, the Nine Night ceremony is called a "set-up" because of the long vigils that take place. Songs

are sung to cheer the family of the deceased, and a musical instrument called the dinky minny is played. The following description of the dinky minny comes from a fisherman, Rupert DaCosta.

Vaudou Ceremony. The American Center of Haitian Art, Matlacha, Florida.

You take a quarter of the green bamboo, young and full of life. Cut when the moon is full, but not before, or it will make a weak sound. Saw a bowstring out of the green skin of the bamboo; wedge it tight at either end to make a bridge. Then cut two straight branches off a guava tree; these will be used for drumsticks. Get a gourd, a calabash, cut a hole at one end to make the resonator. The dinky minny is played with one man on a side; one makes the melody with the gourd, the other beats the rhythm with the sticks.

On a traditional Nine Night, the dinky minny rattles and rasps, clicks and clacks, wails a grief-haunted song on the bamboo bowstrings. While the dinky minny shrieks, children play an African stone-passing game—a stone is passed in a circle to the fast beat of the drum. The rule is that the stone must not be dropped. This is also a time for riddles, jokes, old stories, remembrances of the deceased.

We attended a set-up on Firefly Hill overlooking Port Maria on the north coast of Jamaica. The deceased had been the butler of the English playwright and actor Noël Coward, who lived in Jamaica, off and on, from the late 1940s until his death in 1973. The set-up took place just below Coward's gravesite. The area around the old Coward house is considered haunted, but we saw no duppies that night. The bedroom of the deceased butler was arranged as if he were still there. Coward memorabilia, engulfed in handpicked tropical flowers, was on display. We sat in semi-darkness listening to the songs of the tree frogs and sipping a sweet traditional tea made from the ganja leaf. Halfway through the night, feeling the easy flow of generous feelings that came from all who had gathered, we listened to a woman express the beauty of a life lived to the fullest in a beloved place: "It is very beautiful to live and to love in the place you love best; it is also beautiful to die there."

At another set-up, this one held in Highgate, testimonials were given under the large-leaved cocoa trees. An old man said: "He left the world with more friends than when he entered it." Someone else said: "He shared what he had, when he had it." After the burial the next morning, the will was read and, jarringly, the mystic moment of Nine Night disappeared, overcome by the world-weary act, the struggle, of staying alive. How much easier, we thought, during those euphoric Nine Nights, to be there, perhaps, in spirit only.

OBEAH

At midnight, when the last stroke of the bell died away, the Obeah man slit the throat of the goat—one sharp half-smothered cry, then silence. The blood spurt from the wicked wound splashed onto the head of the girl Susanna; red blood in the bright glare of the fire, as the fountain spilt like wine and her eyes tried to see what lay beyond in the darkness. The Obeah man thinned the fire and made the tranced girl hop over a bar of crimson coals; once, twice, thrice. Then she stood, fixed in place, a dream in her eyes, slowly fading, quietly dimming. In what was left of the fire, he shook out the rest of the blood, which spattered her white dress like a brief settling of rain. "The work done," he panted, his face shining with sweat as hers was dripping with blood. The spell was gone.

—— FROM JAMAICA JOURNAL, BY HUMPHREY FELTON
    INSTITUTE OF JAMAICA ARCHIVE

I know a man, wicked of ways, woke one night
in the March month, the long day month, hear three notes of the
ash-color bird, the one with the red beak, the chick-mon-chick,
that said he'd soon be dead.
I know a man, wicked of ways, take a green lizard
with a saw tail, grind that tail into powder,
mix the powder with wisdom weed to make his
lover vex.
I know a man, wicked of ways, watch two mongoose
pull a snake at either end, stretch him to
death.
I know a man, wicked of ways, who meet the rolling calf
on the Queen's Highway; it roll and bawl and burst
into flame, until the man draw a figure eight in the dirt,
plant a knife in the heart of it, freeze that rolling

calf right there in its flaming tracks.
I know a man, wicked of ways, see a mouse eat a whole
plumcake; remember then, all that's white-white
is sweet-sweet . . . but so deadly.
I know a man, wicked of ways, go up into the bush
at midnight, spread a white sheet under a silk cotton tree,
wait for the moon white blossom fall on the sheet;
when it fall, he can't see it.
I know a man, wicked of ways, make a love chain out of roses
put it round his lover's bed at night, when she wake
she love him more, and leave him less.
I know a man, wicked of ways, send his worst enemy a batch
of cowitch in the mail; and when he open that package,
he itch like hell.
I know a man, wicked of ways, send his worst enemy, the one
who sent him the cowitch he's still itching from, a sweet
potato pie cooked with pufferfish poison, unripe ackee,
stinging grouper, poison barra, moses in the bullrush
and Judy Pussy.
I know a man, wicked of ways, who dead.
—*FROM DUPPIES, DRUM TALK, & OBEAH MEN, BY GERALD*
HAUSMAN AND RAY GRIFFIN

Duppy Pulling Ceremony, Jamaica.
Archive of the Institute of
Jamaica. Rendering by Mariah
Fox.

A possible origin of the word "obeah" is the Akan language's
"obayi" or *"bayi,"* meaning sorcerer. Brought to the Caribbean by
the Ashanti people of West Africa, obeah has flourished for more
than four hundred years. It was, and is, worked by both male and
female practitioners. The origin of obeah is obscure, yet West Indian storytellers explain that in ancient times, every village in Africa
had an obeah man (or woman), who was needed in times of war,
but rarely in times of peace. Obeah was, therefore, a mystical force
of "black magic," which had less focus or purpose during peaceful
times when a village might have only an occasional need for such
power, as in a time of drought; in a sense, a warfare of the gods.
During periods of peace the practitioner in ascendance was the
maye, myalist, myal man. This person was a user of "white magic,"
whose job it was to preside over births, deaths, and so on, on which
daily investments of good luck or ritual blessing were required.

Today many islands still rely on these two practitioners, though the myalist is harder to find and often tends to be a woman. Known as a Captain, Mother, or Shepherd, the myalist is frequently connected with herbal medicine—bush lore—as well as with the Christian revival church. As a medium for the spirit world, the myalist is said to have access to divine cures, literally, the food of the gods. The curative plant medicines found in ancient Africa are available, for the most part, on many of the Caribbean Islands today.

The figure of the frog or toad is common to both obeah and Haitian vaudou. *Bufano marinus,* the toad called frog on the islands, is crushed and dried, then made into a powder. In vaudou rites this powder is mixed with that of a dried, ground-up puffer fish. Once combined, the two create a toxin, which, when added to other unknown ingredients, makes an anaesthetic that can immobilize a person, thus creating what has been popularly called a zombie.

Obeah does not rely as much on chemical potions as voodoo, but it utilizes psycho-suggestive power, the placebo effect of chemical agents—which frequently turn out to be tap water. And it relies heavily on hypnosis and dream control.

The following is a Jamaican description of an "obeah attack":

I came home from work late one night and got into bed. Within a few minutes I heard something flopping on my zinc roof. Once inside my one-room house, the thing jumped on my bed and tried to suffocate me. It was a frog, sent by an obeah man. I killed it by clubbing it with a boot. But then I had to clean up the floor really well because those frogs are full of poison. I saw a chicken eat one one time, and that chicken died a miserable death.

In 1988, while gathering material for this book, we visited an obeah man in Highgate, Jamaica. The obeah man's name was Sweet Pea and he was a short, fat, unattractive man whose "office" was in back of a bar tended by his wife. To meet the man, we first had to meet his wife, who decided whether we were worthwhile clients, that is, if we had any money. When she determined that we did, she showed us the way to his door behind the bar. There was a long queue of people, perhaps as many as twenty-five, stretched out under the almond trees.

Sweet Pea's wife had told him that there were some people "on important business," so he ushered us into his little room immediately. We sat at a lace-covered table. On all of the walls of the room were shelves laden with plastic, fired clay, and porcelain icons. Pets, saints, virgins, even Batman and Robin had their place of honor. These were used, we had heard, for ceremonial purposes; to bless or curse someone. In short order, we found out that a modern obeah man, especially a good one—and Sweet Pea was quite good—works the way a psychiatrist does. After listening to your problem, he presents a possible cure, one that, should you wish to employ him, is certain to work favorably.

And what things could he do?

He could do anything from securing a lost passport to damaging the eyesight of someone—a policeman, or even another obeah man—who was trying to "see" into your life.

In some cases, he might merely act as a sounding board, listening and offering consultation. In other instances, he might prepare a love potion for one who was unlucky in love, or pronounce a death sentence, a curse, on someone who was seeking to injure his client.

We explained to Sweet Pea that we needed to find out who had stolen a wedding ring. (In fact, our host, Bill, back in Port Maria, had lost it while diving on the reef.) So then Sweet Pea took a gold ring off his finger, tied it to a string, and wrapped the string around a pencil. Fetching a glass of water, he placed the ring in the glass, and began a recitation of the names of various saints.

"You see," he explained, "the ring symbolizes marriage, a divine state of union. I ask the saints who preside over relationships to bless this investigation. Now you may ask this ring who took your host's wedding ring."

"How do we do that?"

"You must say: 'By the true and living god who made us all, did

Toad Motif. Art and photograph by Bobbe Besold.

so-and-so take the ring?' Then you just name whoever you think did this thing, and keep repeating the same phrase before each name."

One of our party, Reeve, did this for several minutes, until, when he whispered a certain name, the ring began to chime against the glass.

"There it is," Sweet Pea exclaimed, "the one who stole your wedding ring. That will be seven hundred dollars, Jamaican."

Later, on the way home, we asked Reeve what name he'd mentioned—too softly for any of us to hear—and he said, "Why Bill's, of course."

PARADISE

Above this world there is a door into the unknown, a place where the dialogue between the deity and the earth-born has its celestial origin. Paradise is thus the dawn above the clouds, a mystic sphere alive with promise, but according to the old tales, very much like the world of sticks and stones and broken bones that we have always called home.

The Giryama believe that all things proceed from the marriage of heaven and earth. The Congo people regard heaven as the father and earth as the mother. It is, therefore, a male presence, essence of sun and lion, who presides above, his identity grafted spiritually into the sky itself, as in the North American Indian belief in Father Sky.

To the Baronga of Delagoa Bay, the word *"tilo,"* for paradise or heaven, means not merely the visible sky, but the spiritual principle thus embodied. It is a place, but more than that, it is a presence, which, when activated, "can kill and make alive." Thus the unmoved mover, the deity in abstract repose.

In the Ashanti tale of Nyankopong, the high god of the sky, was originally an earth being. An old woman, they say, was pounding fufu, mashed yams, for her supper when she received a complaint from Nyankopong, who was standing near her. "Why do you always bang against me with your pestle?" he asked. And she, elbow pumping and having nothing to say to this, continued with her work. Put off by the old woman's rudeness, Nyankopong stated: "Because of you, I am going up to the sky."

Now the old woman was much annoyed by his departure because she had wanted to remain in the company of Nyamko-pong. Therefore, she instructed her grandchildren: "Pile these mud bricks, one upon another, until you reach all the way to Nyankopong." The grandchildren did as told, but when they reached the top of the sky and were in sight of Nyankopong, they called down to the old woman. "We have gone as far as possible and we have used all of our bricks." The old woman called up, "Take one from the bottom and put it on the top." They did this, and the edifice tumbled from the sky, killing all who fell and all who lay below.

The same story, biblically molded, is that of the Tower of Babel. A Jamaican storyteller, Roy McKay, once explained that all men were brothers at one time, and that the downfall came not as a fall from grace or a plucking of the sexual fruit of Eden, but rather in the piling up of bricks in the tower that was to place man ever closer to God. "This," the storyteller urged, "was man's mistake, his vanity, to try to gaze upon the face of God. So his structure to heaven fell on him and after that, all men spoke different lan-guages, and all that we know today, is blah, blah, blah and boom, boom, boom."

When Homer Smith, the African American hero of the novel, *Lilies of the Field,* by William E. Barrett, visits his first Catholic church, in the desert of Arizona, he, being a deep Southern Bap-tist, is less amused than alarmed. "There were vague memories in his mind about tales he had heard of weird Catholic spells and of idol worship, but he was curious about the structure of the build-ing." The priest explains to Homer that underneath the outer coating of mud plaster there were the bricks that made the church. "They are simple bricks," he said. "They are made of adobe clay and a little straw, sometimes the manure of the horse, then dried in the sun."

Somehow, Homer hears in the priest's words and sees in the sun-drenched, mud-hardened clay a parable of his own life: from dust to dust. "I am glad I saw your church," he says. And then the

Background: Paradise Tree, Baobab, Africa. Photograph by Ross LewAllen.

priest says the thing that makes his humble house of mud and straw a pristine version of the fallen tower: "It is a poor church, but God comes down to it." Not man going up, but God coming down; for, it was the great fear of the African ancestor spirits, the Orakuru, that brazen man should climb up into heaven and make himself at home there.

If the road to heaven is not an easy one to traverse, as the Ashanti and the Bible often illustrate, then, perhaps it is not a road at all; perhaps it is not a route, but a paradox. Often, in African legend, it is, rather than a road, a tree, in which a road or a path appears only at the end. The Wachaga of Kilimanjaro live near the mountain that is, metaphorically, closer to God than any other prominence of Africa—closer, in fact, than most of the rest of the world as well. This is their story, "The Heaven Tree":

Once there was a girl by the name of Kichalundo. One day she went out to cut grass and fell into a marshy bog. In no time, she sank like a stone, finding herself falling into a strange region of middle earth. There grew, thereafter, a tree in the place where Kichalundo disappeared. It came out of the earth and sprang into the sky. Such a lovely tree it was, that boys from the village would come to lie about in its generous shade and cattle would graze beneath the great length of its shadow.

There came a day when some boys, playing in the branches of the tree, decided to climb higher, and higher. "Where are you going?" their companions called to them. "We are climbing to the Wuhuu," they cried back. Now, the Wuhuu was the great world above where-on the Wahuu, the heaven clan, were said to live. And, still further, they traveled, all the way to the Waranjui, those ennobled beings who live above the sky. Pity the lowly two-legged people, the tale concludes, who must live so far from heaven, so close to the middle earth of the dead.

In the Chaga version of the story "Three Women by the River," the spirit road, trail, and tree involves, as in the Cabala, a series of rites of passage, which, in this case, involve demonstrable manners. The story tells of a woman whose baby is despised by two

Haitian Art. The American Center of Haitian Art, Matlacha, Florida. Photograph by R. D. Johnson.

other women, who also have babies with them. All three are washing at the river, when the two unwell-wishers decide on a deadly trick. Hiding their babies behind some broad leaves, they call to the third mother, their friend, and say: "We have thrown away our children, why don't you do the same?"

"Where have you thrown them?" asks the third.

"In the river," they reply.

Whereupon, the third throws her baby into the river, where it is immediately devoured by a crocodile. In tears the desperate mother climbs the tallest tree by the riverbank. And she climbs far into the sky. After much climbing, she meets a tribe of leopards, who grace the dark green leaves with their black spots and their long, golden bodies.

"Where are you going?" the leopard people ask.

"I am going to Mulungu," she answers, pausing in her climb.

The leopards are sufficiently pleased with the woman's gentle manner, and they direct her to the birds named nsenzi. The birds, also gratified by her politeness, send her on to the large fish named Mazomba. In each visit, the woman's righteousness is recognized by her fellow creatures. And so she finally meets Mulungu, who, seeing her goodness, calls forth the crocodile who ate her baby and immediately restores the infant to life.

So it is that *tilo,* or paradise, rewards those whom it treasures. It is, in effect, not a path at all, but a place where one may have dialogue with the deities. It is often said that the higher you go, the thinner the air, the rarer the atmosphere. The Elizabethans described these upward-flowing arcs to heaven as ethereal realms, each of which was inhabited by one order of an ascending hierarchy of angelic personages.

The Wachaga believe that the highest of Mother Earth's offerings is the snowfield at the top of Kilimanjaro. This, they say, is inhabited by a tribe of elf people, whose ladders gleaming in the sun, go into the world above. "Where is the kraal of the moon?" asks Mrile, who, spinning on a stool, goes flying up into the ether to meet "Heaven Folk." Surprisingly, they are not unlike himself. These are people who work in the field, as he does; who cut wood and dig ditches and gather crops and prepare meals.

Why, Mrile asks himself, do these Heaven Folk not cook their food? And he finds, suddenly, that they are less like him than he thought, for they have no fire. Taking out his fire sticks, he presents them with the gift of flame, proving that paradise is less perfect than the world in which we live, and that divinity is incomplete without materiality.

There is a place above Mount Kilimanjaro
where the gods dream, and it is called,
because men dream too, paradise.
But that place—where kindness is kept
and scorn is burned—is in the heart,
and it is no dream, it is real.
That is why people try so hard to find
it: Because it is theirs by birthright,
because it is in them, because they know
it has no geographical bearing
because it is reached only by the ladder of love.
—*KELVIN RODRIQUES*

QUILT

Put your hands to work—
and your heart to God.
—*OLD SHAKER ADAGE*

Fabric scraps, old clothes, bought goods, and threads; these are things that make up a quilt. It is a bird's nest made of storytelling panels, a tale of beginnings and sometimes endings, and, always, journeys. The colors and shapes of African wisdom leap and jump in the quilter's art. And the quilter seems to say, "My children, my grandchildren, and even their grandchildren, will sleep under the watchful stars of this blanket and under the purple crescent moons that I have put here for as long as the thread will hold." The African-American poet Terri Lynne Singleton tells of the perfect pattern in the following essay and poem:

The soft, melodic voice came from behind, catching my ear, stopping my eyes. "These old hands," she whispered, "made that." I look from the quilt hanging before me and the photo essay about the quiltmaker and see that I am speaking with the "stitcher" of this wonder. This quilt! My second trip to an exhibit of African-American quilters and I linger again in front of my easy favorite. The quilt that made me smile in recognition, stroll away, drew me back, always saying, "Here I am, I'm talking to you."

Drawn to this collection of fabric scraps, old clothes, new "bought" goods, and thread, I walk from panel to panel and learn new lessons. Self-taught, it is rare that I see a grouping of quilts stitched by African-Americans. Rarer still that they are hung as a complete show. They all speak to me of hard lives and soft babies sheltered beneath. Home and the families they've warmed, often passed from one generation of brown hands to another. Packed in trunks, carried in cardboard luggage on the bus trip north. A collection of fabric scraps that say, "This is back home, no matter how far you travel from us." "Go 'head," she encourages me. "You can touch it." My eyes slide to the "No Touching" placards posted every third quilt. She verbally nudges me, "It's mine, it's all right, go on."

Smooth cottons play with my fingertips. The colors and shapes of African mythology and cosmology leap and jump from the black background. Gold sun, red snake, green and white trees. Two large, brown hands reach down from the sun's rays and brown hands ring the border with purple crescent moons and blue stars dancing within the palms. I tell her that her quilt puts me in mind of the two biblical theme quilts by Harriet Powers, born a slave in 1837, dying free, a stitcher whose quilts now hang in the Smithsonian Institution and the Museum of Fine Arts, Boston. Her quilts, I say, are fine art, as Harriet Powers's quilts are. She quietly chuckles. "Art! No, child, these bedcovers. All my children slept under this, one time or another. Glad you like it, though. You stitch?"

We speak of quilting and stitching, bedcovers and art, working from patterns or "stitchin' what you know." She explains the brown hands emerging from the sun are God's; the smaller, around the border, represent family. Crescent moons for those "still with us" and stars for family "passed on." We talk of Jesus and God: "Some folks say he's a white man, but we stitch what we know . . . am I right?" Suddenly remembering my manners, I turn to introduce myself; she has quietly slipped away. I darted quickly, exhibit room to exhibit room, searching for the voice, the hands that had stitched as many years as I've been walking.

Weeks later, a small notice appears in the arts section of my local newspaper noting that the quilt exhibition is moving on. I decided to visit the quilts one last time.

Background: Ekpe Secret Society Cloth. 20th Century African; Igbo, Nigeria. The Lowe Art Museum, University of Miami.

As I buy the book about the exhibit, I mention to the docent seated before me that the quilts I've seen have made my heart very happy. I tell her I was honored to meet the maker of the biblical theme quilt hanging in the second exhibit room. Puzzled, frowning, she gazes at me while pointing in the direction of the quilt.

"You couldn't have," she whispers. "Betsy, the maker of that quilt, died two years ago."

On my way to the quilt, I am stopped by an eager young docent.

"Let me show you my favorite." She proudly stops before Betsy's quilt.

"I'm talking to you," I hear softly from behind me.

"Oh yes," I'm barely able to say, as tears whisper past my eyelids. "This one I've met."

We call your name, Harriet Powers:

two of your five children, born not of your womb, but of your hands, imagination, heart. Stitched as you lived under slavery, one later sold away from you, traveling in your lap, in my flour sack covering. Moving to the home and hands of Jennie Smith in 1890.

We call your name, Harriet Powers:

unable to read or write, you communicate through us of your visual and oral world. A world of the Bible and legends. A universe of the stars and the heavens. We speak for you, of the serpent in the Garden of Eden, Adam's rib, comets, eclipses, the sun, the God you have adopted as your own.

We call your name, Harriet Powers:

living in two museums, the Smithsonian in Washington, D.C., and the Museum of Fine Arts, Boston; we are among the chosen from the Smithsonian quilt collection. Manufactured in China. Quilts and pillow shams based on our faces, sold again in the marketplace. Accompanied by information stating our birth and where we live, neglecting your personal history and name.

We call your name, Harriet Powers:
   that those who prosper from the labor of your hand and heart and
those who rest upon and under your creativity shall know.

We call your name, Harriet Powers:
   across the galleries and halls of the buildings in which we live—
   across the farmland in Buck Branch, Georgia, where you died,
free, in the year 1911—
   across the fields of the plantation you were born to, in 1837 and
on which you toiled till the end of the Civil War—
   across the vast oceans to the homeland of your ancestors—
   we call you home—
   we call that others may hear—
   we call your name—

Harriet Powers

   Harriet Powers

      Harriet Powers
   —TERRI LYNNE SINGLETON

Ekpe Secret Society Cloth. 20th Century African; Igbo, Nigeria. The Lowe Art Museum, University of Miami.

RAP

Shool, shool, shool;
*   I rule!*
Shool, shool, shool;
*   I rule!*
Shool, shacker-rack;
I shool bubba cool!
—THOMAS W. TALLEY, 1922

In 1899, one year before the last millennium, writer Jeanette Robinson Murphy stated in *Popular Science Monthly:*

Fifty years from now, when every vestige of slavery has disappeared, and even its existence has become a fading memory, America, and probably Europe, will suddenly awake to the sad fact that we have irrevocably lost a veritable mine of wealth through our failure to appreciate and study, from a musician's standpoint, the beautiful African music, whose rich stores will then have gone forever from our grasp.

Nearly a century after she wrote this prediction, the facts seem to have turned the other way around. The song elements of African music—what Murphy then called "strange, weird, untamable, barbaric melodies"—are with us still, and to such a degree that they may be said to have influenced almost all other musical forms on the contemporary scene.

And what, in fact, were the untamable barbarisms?

Street Rapper. Nashville, Tennessee. Photograph by Beth Gwynn.

They were deeply religious outpourings based upon field songs, shouts, and hollers of the antebellum South. Before that, of course, they were the intrinsic, trance-inducing, supple soundings of Mother Africa. They were, simply, the voice of the earth. Brought to the "New World," they became imbued with regionalism and biblical lore, for, as Murphy rightly comments: "One of the most persistent fancies the old slaves cherished was that they were the oppressed Israelites, that the Southerners were the cruel Egyptians, and that Canaan was freedom." Ironically—or predictably, perhaps—Rastafarian religion, with its own form of reggae apocalypse, speaks of the same paradigm: The world in which we live is Babylon, aflame.

The sweet honey in the rock that made African American music so popular in the minstrelsies of long ago is what empowers it today. Murphy cites them melodramatically, but, curiously, they apply.

What are they?

First, a breaking up of European phrasing and notation. Just as patois and creole language encoded the secrets of the African tongue, so, naturally, did African singing. The phrase and the breath, then, were the hot wind of the veldt, the stutter and clatter of rain, the sensuous voices of cicadas on the wing. The voice, Murphy reminds, is "exceedingly nasal and undulating"; and around "every prominent note . . . a variety of small notes called 'trimmings' . . . the breath goes on from line to line and from verse to verse, from a high note to a very low one, dividing monosyllabic words in two syllables."

The meditation offered by Murphy is that "the tunes came directly from Africa and were almost supernatural in their hold upon the people." One wonders what she would say about today's rap music; if it is appreciably different in any way, from the African trimmings she spoke of or is just another expression of the same irrepressible spirit.

Corn shuckers on Georgia farms a century ago sang, as they worked, a kind of old-time rap. The "lead rappers" were called generals, and the corn song was sung with a chorus. What the generals gave out, the chorus kept up, rapping along as they shucked. These songs were sung continuously during the entire time the work was going on, the generals and shuckers alternating verses:

FIRST GENERAL: Here is your corn shucker.
ALL HANDS: Oh ho ho ho ho.
SECOND GENERAL: Here is your nigger ruler.
ALL HANDS: Oh ho ho ho ho.
FIRST GENERAL: Don't you hear me holler?
ALL HANDS: Oh ho ho ho ho.

In this way the generals were able to recount adventures, travels, and experiences common to everyone, or perhaps particular to one, yet interesting to all. The famous Hare trickster of Africa, who became Brer Rabbit, on the one hand, and Bugs Bunny, on the other, trips blithely into the corn shucker's repertoire:

GENERALS: Rabbit in the garden.
CHORUS: Rabbit hi oh.
GENERALS: Dog can't ketch him.
CHORUS: Rabbit hi oh.
GENERALS: Gun can't shoot him.
CHORUS: Rabbit hi oh.
GENERALS: Man can't skin him.
CHORUS: Rabbit hi oh.
GENERALS: Cook can't cook him.
CHORUS: Rabbit hi oh.
GENERALS: Folks can't eat him.
CHORUS: Rabbit hi oh.

Corn songs of the Deep South were syncopations and ruminations that went into the mythic past and the perilous or humorous present. They were beaten out, shucked out, and passed on,

Background: Mad Skillz. Courtesy Big Beat/Atlantic. Photograph by Daniel Hastings.

down, and all around. As entertainment and education, they often spoke of the slave's own plight, giving advice and a residual stream of wisdom that pitted man's morals against an essentially hostile universe. They were rough sport, wrested from the daily grind of a hard day's work under the sun; and yet, all things considered, they were an unmistakable form of early rap poetry.

Facing page: Mista Grimm. New Deal Music/550 Music. Photograph by Chi Modu.

RIVER

By the rivers of Babylon
Where we sat down
And there we wept
When we remembered Zion;
For the wicked carried us away to
Captivity and required of us a song;
But how can we be singing
In a strange land?
—RASTAFARIAN CHANT

And yet the river was crossed and the song was sung: A song of freedom with voices raised in unison. A song of captivity, and longing: A song of remembering. The meaning comes pure and clean, bright as light, in the adaptation of this lovely biblical psalm. Babylon, the city of selfishness and thus idolatry, becomes a symbol of a people's suffering and humiliation. Zion, the city of holiness and fulfilled dreams, the place of deliverance, becomes a mythical mind-city. The wicked with their cargoes of human flesh are the piratical slavers who traversed the Middle Passage and deposited African people on the new continent, the strange land.

The Negro spiritual "The Water Is Wide" tells of a different body of water, across which only love may pass:

The water is wide
I can't cross over
And neither have I

09371. A SOUTHERN BAPTISM.

wings to fly
Build me a boat
That can carry two
And both shall row
My love and I.

Southern Baptism. From the Collections of the Library of Congress.

Looking back over that great water, what do we see? We must look past the ancestor on the auction block, past the shackled foot, the head bent in shame. We must cross over and rediscover the old discovered country. The task is to build the boat of the only substance that will not give way to storm, to fury. Our task, as so many prophets have said, is to build the boat out of love.

Noah, they say, was once the architect of such a boat. And lest anyone think him a creation of literature and the human imagination, there is a time-veiled tradition in Bornu, an old African kingdom on a plain that is now part of Nigeria, which states that Noah came from there. "Bornu" means, in fact, "the Country of Noah." The vast tableland lies near Lake Chad; on it some say, Noah's family disembarked. The natural diversity of the creatures that have lived there for so many centuries lends support to the myth, for the land is loud with lions, giraffes, elephants, crocodiles, hippopotami, hyenas, gazelles, ostriches, and antelope. Bornu, a land once cursed, now blessed, by water.

What of that other Africa, the so-called *dark* continent? What shadows stir in the ruffled curtains of green; what measure of ancestor lies hidden there? Peering through his mask of memory, looking out across the great water, poet Nicolas Guillén heard heavy muffled gongs, shadows that only he could see:

> I am dying
>   *(says my black grandfather)*
> Black water of crocodiles,
> green morning of coco palms.
> I am weary
>   *(says my white grandfather)*
> O sails of bitter wind
> galleon burning gold.
> I am dying
>   *(says my black grandfather)*
> O coasts of virgin throats
> cheated with glass trinkets
> I am weary
>   *(says my white grandfather)*

Boy and Boat, Okavango Delta. Photograph by Barbara Baumann.

Those who did not die and would not allow themselves the luxury of growing weary, "He who fights and runs away/lives to fight another day" (Bob Marley). In America, some came, at the end of their running, to the great river they had heard so much about. So great was its breadth that the moon slept on its breast, and points of grass grew like pin feathers upon it; and the Indians called the endless river Pa-hay-okee, the Grassy Water, the Everglades.

To the Everglades, then, came the slaves known as Maroons (from the Spanish *cimarron,* wild), who were, in fact, round-faced Senegalese from Dakar, Ebos, Egbas, and the feared, hard-eyed Ashanti. Marooned in America, sold into slavery, these men refused chains and took to the old Indian trails. And so, soot-black, brown-black, blue-black, and black-black, they met the red people of the great grass-quaking river. The Mikasukis (Miccosukee) and the Calusas had little to do with them. But the Seminoles, who were originally members of the Creek Nation and whose name in Muskogee means free-man, let the blacks be with them. As Marjory Stoneman Douglas points out in *The Everglades: River of Grass:*

Besides, the Negro had a great deal to add to the Indian way of life, especially his agelong preoccupation with agriculture, which made him always a harder everyday worker, on his own land, than the migratory hunting Indians. The Negro's never sufficiently recognized legal shrewdness, which in Africa had produced his system of tribal courts, with his practical gifts of gab, argument and windy eloquence, which the Indians call "nigger wit," were to serve for well or ill the councils of his Indian allies, masters and relatives. He fought more fiercely even than the Indian. He had more to lose.

In time, the bloodlines of red and black were no longer separate. However, when word traveled, at the close of the eighteenth century, that all slave ships putting into Bahamian ports were impounded and their cargoes freed, a Native American medicine man named Scipio Bowlegs fled the slave catchers off the coast of Florida. The great water was no barrier to him and his Maroons. These were Seminoles "with some African blood," whose lives were inseparable from the water on which they lived. Arriving in the Bahamas, they planted corn, peas, and pumpkins, which they had brought with them, and they kept largely to themselves. Four years later, the only vestiges of their Native American heritage were their well-made bows and arrows and their preference for living in log cabins.

The image of the river lies long upon the human imagination; for our thoughts are borne on a river and they move like rafts between the islands of the mind:

> *And afterwards we would watch the lonesomeness of the river, and kind of lazy along, and by and by lazy off to sleep. . . . Sometimes we'd have that whole river all to ourselves for the longest time. . . . We had the sky up there, all speckled with stars, and we used to lay on our backs and look up at them, and discuss about whether they was made or only just happened. Jim, he allowed they was made, but I allowed they happened. . . . We used to watch the stars that fell, too, and see them streak down. Jim allowed they'd got spoiled and was hove out of the nest.*

Mark Twain knew well what the Mississippi was, and how the great firmament overarched it at night. But it was not for Huck to animate the stars, or to personify them. This was the job of Jim, the African mythmaker, who knew that all above was also below; that all things are possessed of immutable life. To Jim the river was more than moving water; it was the stuff of dreams, magic, morality, wisdom, retribution, redemption, sorrow, and suffering. To Jim there were waterways known and unknown, remembered and unremembered; vast and secret tributaries of the human heart:

Rivers of silt and salt
of sun and rain
of shadow and shade
of light, dark, heat, spark

Rivers that speak
and having spoken
speak on

Rivers of meeting and mating
wondering and wandering
longing and lingering
lessening and thinning

Rivers of ravers, rovers, lovers
and losers.
Rivers of answers
no one knows . . .

—FROM DUPPIES, DRUM TALK & OBEAH MEN, *BY GERALD HAUS-*
   MAN AND RAY GRIFFIN

ROCK

An ancient African method of settling family as well as tribal disputes was to draw a line in the dirt, set up opposing parties on either side of the line, and, at a given signal, to begin throwing rocks. In the Caribbean, this is still a common practice. There is a frightful silence in the drawing of the line, as if it represented much more than life and death, as if it meant the continuation of the species. And in the raising of the fateful stones: A biblical stillness is there, too.

It seems that much that is African comes from the symbolism of the rock, or as they say in the islands, the "rock-stone." Selvin Johnson, a folk singer, once sang a song about a man whose mornings are spent in a gully, hammering big rocks into littler ones. The sound of his musical hammer rings upon the tree-lined ridge; he is imprisoned by the rocks he breaks into little pieces as paving for roads—white stones sunk in black tar. Johnson's "man-a-bruk-stone" song has in it all the travail of being black, of life's work spent like Sisyphus' in the thankless task of being born and suffering, and dying.

John Henry, the great rock-breaker, soul-cleaver, died "with a hammer in his hand," having broken through a rock mountain and beaten a steam drill, but paying with his life for his legendary effort. However, he proved that a man with a brave heart is better than a machine with an oil-driven motor. It is still said in the hills of West Virginia and the river bottoms of west Texas that John Henry was a real man, though whether light or dark, large or small, no one seems to remember:

His hammer rang like silver and shined like gold:
That old hammer killed John Henry;
But it didn't kill me,
Lord, it didn't kill me.

The steel-driving man lives on as a kind of Christ in black armor, his death providing life for all who would listen to the story.

There is, of course, the biblical tale of the Rock, retold here as a black folktale:

It seems that Jesus and his disciples were walking along one day when Jesus told everybody to pick up a rock. They did as he said, all except Peter, who picked up a little pebble and put it in his side pocket.

Now, as they walked along the eleven disciples kept switching the rocks from hand to hand. At the end of the day, they had reached the Sea of Galilee, and Jesus told them to fish awhile. They caught many fish and cooked them and Christ said: "Now bring up your rocks." So they brought up their rocks and Jesus turned them into loaves—all except Peter's. His little pebble was too small to make into much of anything.

A few days later, Jesus told his disciples they were going for anoth-er walk, and to take up some more rocks. Each man picked up a rock—all except Peter. He tore down half a mountain. It was so big he could not move it with his hands. All day long he sweated before that big rock mountain; but, by the end of the day, Jesus told them to sit down and bring up their rocks.

Everyone came forward but Peter. He was still working at the mountain, trying to get it to move. Well, finally, he brought it up to Jesus, huffing and puffing, all out of breath. And Jesus told Peter, "I am going to build my church on your rock here." But Peter caught his breath and said, "No, sir; you're going to turn my rock into bread!"

Now Jesus knew that Peter meant what he said, so he turned

Peter's rock into a mountain of bread, and that was the bread that fed 5,000. Then he took up the other eleven rocks his disciples gave him and these he glued together and built his church upon. And that is why the Christian church is split up into so many different kinds, because it's built on a pieced-up rock.

The rock is perhaps the oldest of symbols; one that, like the church, we have built many others upon. Going back in time, we have evidence of this, sometimes literally rather than figuratively. The lively monochromes, the South African rock pictures, are among the oldest records of human activity on earth. These ancient artworks depict running, lunging, flying figures, a tableau of cartoonlike abstractions mostly created several thousand years ago, although some were executed within the living memory of man. Motifs of fire, rain, stars, the elemental actors in the drama of humankind, share the role of spirit of creation, celebrating the poetry of the hunt, the prayer of thanks that follows.

Above: Inmates at Reed Camp, Angola, Louisiana, 1935. *From the Collections of the Library of Congress.*
Background: South Chicago Baptist Church. From the Collections of the Library of Congress.

In the black folk song "Sinner Man," it is the end of the world, and not the beginning, in which, once again, the Rock is mentioned.

> *O, Sinner Man, where you gonna run to?*
> *Run to the Rock, but the Rock can't hide you.*

Peter Tosh recast the song, calling it "Downpresser Man," but the lyrics are essentially the same: The Rock, no matter how large or strong, cannot hide an evil man from his fate. We do not have to go to the caves of South Africa to bear witness. We merely have to look at the concrete bunkers, the modern-day caves where men still cast their fiery, frenetic glances, writing cryptic phrases that repeatedly croak: *I am.*

SERPENT

Sitting in a hot bus in the heat of the day in Kingston, Jamaica, we hear a child's voice on JBC Radio:

> *The snake has eyes of glass;*
> *the snake comes and coils itself round a pole;*
> *with his eyes of glass, round a pole,*
> *with his eyes of glass.*
> *The snake walks without legs;*
> *the snake hides in the grass;*
> *walking he hides in the grass*
> *walking without legs.*

The child's voice is infinitely sweet amid the rubble and rumble of downtown Kingston. Splintered glass winks from the sidewalk; an old woman limps grotesquely across the road. What is so sweet about this child-voice, singing of a serpent? Is it that the old African spirit is not yet quenched? And we hear it so clearly—the pre-biblical grace of the thing that is feared, and therefore loved, for the strong feeling thus generated. As we wind our way home through the Junction Road of a thousand turns, the Wog Water River far below us, shimmering like snake scales in the late afternoon light, the young voice comes on the radio once more:

> *Dead snake cannot eat;*
> *dead snake cannot hiss;*

cannot walk
cannot run.
Dead snake cannot look;
dead snake cannot drink,
cannot breathe,
cannot bite.

Serpent Motif. Art and photograph by Bobbe Besold.

Some mornings later, we're walking down a garden path in Port Maria and there is a dead boa constrictor directly in our path. It is gray like the sea at dawn, pearly and soft. The watchful eyes that never sleep are sewn shut in death. Half the body is alive with ants, the ones Jamaicans call pity-me-little. Our friend Morris sees us looking at the snake, and he says: "There is a big one of them in the hills where you run every day."

"How big?"

He smiles. "Twenty, twenty-five feet."

"Have you seen it?"

He shakes his head. "Me smell him, mon."

"What does a snake that big smell like?"

"Rotten eggs." He grins.

For weeks after that, we look about in the bush, parting the banana leaves that hide the path looking for the snake with eyes of glass that hides in the grass, and when dead, cannot die.

In Port-au-Prince, Haiti, there is a little eden of thirty acres. It is sacred land, a symbol of hope. Here, the vaudou priests come to beat drums, and the leaf doctors, natural healers, seek the seven-leaf plant that cures illness. Outside the garden, garbage rots in the sun. More than 96 percent of the island is deforested, and when it rains, the mud slides are treacherous. The garden is nearly all that is left.

The drummers drum, the healers hum. Chain-smokers drink rum. The open-air vaudou temple called Vallée des Serpents beckons the root doctors and leaf carriers who come from miles away to fill their prescriptions. The garden's walls are crumbling. The air smells fresh within, but outside, the city smells of fetor and death.

One night, two nights, three nights.

On the fourth night of vaudou, there is a great tea-tasting. The one-legged drummer named Petienne Joudion lifts everyone's spirits. He has played in the cabarets of Paris; he now thumps his drum in the garden of promise, in Port-au-Prince.

"Everything here is sacred," someone says. "It all belongs to the Snake God, Damballah."

On the fifth night of voodoo, the god is sought.

Are there snakes here . . . real, not spirit, snakes?

In the morning, there is a piercing scream. Someone has seen a snake. No, not one, two. There are two boa constrictors, splashing in the toilet of the house that is buried in the garden.

What is the meaning of this?

Facing page: Masai Warriors with Serpent Bracelets (designed by Laura LewAllen). Photograph by Ross LewAllen.

The garden, they say, is alive. It will heal the sickness around it, the cinder of a city that smolders in the immensity of its own poverty.

The old gods come when called, they say.

They come to the garden, as in the days of old.

And one of them, Damballah, is the Serpent Father, the healer who cannot die. Call him Quetzalcoatl or St. Patrick—these are both names locked within this love—or Damballah. Call him rainbow, smoke, the great umbilical cord of life. Call him Tail-Swallower. Call him Connector of Earth and Sky. Whatever you call him, he will always be there, for that is his most prominent mystery at the top of the hierarchy of the gods. According to Karen McCarthy Brown, author of *Mama Lola: A Vodou Priestess in Brooklyn:* "As a coiling sinuous serpent, he is a persistent, unquenchable life force that unites past and present and turns both into a future that is and is not different from the past."

SHOUT

Shout to the gathering!
African tunes and songs, the
Ancestor of spirituals.
Shout to the heavens!
Spirituals, the descendant of
The shout.
Shout to the one up above!
—*TERRI LYNNE SINGLETON*

The traditional African shout is a primal celebration of the human voice raised in song, chant, call, cry, formal praise and confirmation. It is, moreover, the link to African possession dances practiced by priests and healers. Shouting is the physical expression of African tunes and songs containing pure religious fervor. African-American slaves, according to Zora Neale Hurston, "danced in the ring shout—with the result that the lyrics of the songs were acted out or dramatized by the band of shouters."

The biblical reference to the great power of the shout may be found in Joshua, chapter six, wherein the gates of Jericho are tightly shut, the city locked. The Lord explains to Joshua that the city, no matter how impregnable, shall be his for the shouting. Not a single word shall be spoken until the command is given by Joshua; then comes the earth-shattering shout that brings down the walls of Jericho. It is no wonder, then, that African-American slaves, steeped in their own shouting tradition, fell to the hyp-

Children Playing, Eatonville, Florida. Photograph by Zora Neale Hurston. From the Collections of the Library of Congress.

notic tone of this biblical verse, reaffirming what they already knew.

Shouting has always been a shared experience—a synergy between preacher and congregant. It is also, on many Caribbean islands, a way of communicating over great distances, a reaching across space with the human voice. It is question and answer, wonder and certainty; and it is passed from person to person.

African shouting, as well as congregational shouting, has been explained, by Hurston as "an emotional explosion, responsive to rhythm. It is called forth by: (1) sung rhythm; (2) spoken rhythm; (3) humming rhythm; (4) the foot-patting or hand-clapping that imitates very closely the tom-tom."

The following participatory shout was written by Terri Lynne Singleton for two voices. One voice takes the lefthand part, the other the righthand part. Read from top to bottom; lines at the same level are to be read simultaneously. Begin softly, work to loud—raise voices, clap hands, shout on:

SING PRAISES
A Two-Voice Shout

Praises!

                                    Praises!
Rise up   *Rise up*
Rise up

                                    Rise up
Praises!

                                    Praises!
To Him   *To Him*
And those

                        That came before
Praises!

                                    Praises!
                        Celebrate family

Celebrate home
Sing joy

                                        Sing joy
                                        Sing love
                                        Sing hope
Sing praises!   *Sing praises!*
Ancestors we

                                        Remember
Home

                                        That we love
Family

                                        To celebrate
Praises!   *Praises!*
To Him
That brings

                                        All that came before
Back to
The places

                                        Of joy
                                        Of love
                                        Of hope
Sing praises!   *Sing praises!*

SIGN

Signs are something unnatural (supernatural) in the natural order of things, and they are usually of two kinds, or we might say, of two minds: good and bad. Now, if the sign is good, you just go about your business as before, only with a lot more luck. But if the sign is bad, well, there are charms and cures for everything, if you can just remember them.

Most signs revolve around the season, time and tide, the turning of the moon. In the case of the latter, the days just before or after the new moon are best for birthing, the beginning of life, but this holds equally true for ideas born of the mind, or any beginning thing. Conversely, the full moon marks the summation of something, the time, for instance, to harvest a crop, reap an idea already in fruition.

Dark of the moon is the time to plant such things as roots and tubers because they thrive in darkness. However, flowers and fruits—plants that like bright air—should be put into the earth during the light of the moon. The felling of trees is done in moon-darkness, while the charming of a wart is done in the last quarter of the moon. Obviously, moonlight is a time of certain actions and precautions, a time when lovers and thieves makes trysts and pacts. Cut your hair on the full moon and it will get dry and brittle. Cut it on the new moon and it will grow with the moon.

Rooster Brother. Drawing by Devon Himes, Kansas City Art Institute.

In strong moonlight fruit is full and strong; this is the time to prune and mend and, in affairs of the heart, to make amends. When the moon is in darkness, things may seem to go awry or come apart, but they are also merely awaiting their time of light.

For the African American of long ago, weather sign was seen and sensed, dreamed and visioned, and the old ways were remembered and brought back whenever they applied to something that was happening in the present. Though few could remember why bathing a cat in sulfur water would surely bring rain, it was a common practice; as was hanging a snake, belly up to the sun, in a tree or on a fence. Rain was also sought by sweeping cobwebs from rafters and sprinkling salt on two crossed matches.

Looking for rain sign, rather than making it, was another story altogether. If birds fly in different directions, a storm is coming. If birds burnish their feathers or sing out of turn at night, it means rain sign. When ants bank up their nest, rain is surely coming, and if you want to know when, then all you have to do is count the stars within the circle around the moon, and you will have the number of days before the storm.

Commonplace sign is another way to tell what is going to happen. These are signs of certainty that come from people passing in the street, from hands and gestures and itches. If a woman in the company of men should suddenly sneeze, this is a definite sign of good luck—for one of the men, that is. If a person's palm itches, money is on its way. And if a ladybug lights on your arm, it will bring good luck if you spit on it—but only if the ladybug doesn't return. You are supposed to say, "Ladybug, ladybug, fly away with my good wish, and don't come back with bad news."

Spitting, in general, however, is thought to be dangerous, as in the old adage about spitting in the wind. A Creole saying goes thus: "Spit at someone and you die like a dog." It is also considered treacherous to spit into flame of any kind, but especially a fire, as it will "draw your lungs up."

In the American Southwest, in cotton-picking country, a commonplace sign of good luck was to be able to make love to a

Background: Cotton Pickers. Drawing by Teri Sanders, Kansas City Art Institute.

woman while picking cotton. However, if bolls of white blow across a field in the wind, a snowstorm is on its way. Then again, when a woman stands in a cotton field at night, and sees some cotton coming toward her, it's a sign that she is going to a wedding . . . perhaps her own.

Birds are omens in most cultures; in African folklore they bring good, bad, and abominable luck. Pigeons gathering about a house in Louisiana meant only one thing—good luck coming. But in Jamaica, the song of the chick-mon-chick-bird in the month of March was an omen of death. Conversely, on the same island, a visit from the doctor bird, a hummingbird with a particularly

Cotton Picking, South Carolina.
Photograph by Doris Ulmann.
From the Collections of the
Library of Congress.

long swallowtail (it resembles a nineteenth-century doctor in a frock coat), is always a sign of good health.

In general, African Americans in rural areas believed that a rooster crowing at the back door was a death sign, while the same at the front door was merely visitors coming. If a rooster strutted up to the front steps and crowed three times in succession, that meant you should play the numbers game and win.

Dreams come in all sorts and sizes and their portents are pleasing and perverse, depending upon the specific sign. The old dream of pulling a tooth was a death sign in African-American lore; dreams of horses and turtles were always well-meaning and luck-bringing. Dream-sign advice in the bayou country went as follows: "If you get a love letter, lay it open. Then fold the letter nine different ways. Lastly, pin it to the inside of your shirt over the heart. At night before going to bed, put the letter in your left glove and place this under your pillow. Now, if your lover is true, you will dream of gold or diamonds. But if your lover is false, you will dream of washed clothes or graves."

Life, goes a West Indian song, is all symptom and sign. Believe what you will, things *seen* are greater than things known; and only when things are first seen can they be known later. A Jamaican saying holds that "the heart cannot leap what the eye cannot see." Or, "To feel it is to know it." And the oldest of African proverbs says, "Only when you have crossed the river can you know if the crocodile has a bump on his snout." Such thinking transcends thought and runs counter to the Cartesian pronouncement, "I think, therefore, I am." Sympton and sign declare that the only thinking that needs to be done is by a higher power.

SOUL

Native American tribes believe that there are two separate souls. One, they say, will always reside with the material body. After death this soul becomes one with the earth, with which it is irrevocably bound. The other soul, which may escape us when we dream, is more fluid and transcendent. After death, according to myths, it rises and travels into the realm of sun and star.

The West Indian corollary here is almost an exact reflection. Mackie McDonnough, a bush doctor of Ashanti origin, once said: "We believe there are two souls, one large and one small. The large soul stays with the structure, the body, when you die; the little soul becomes a part of the natural world."

Asked if it was the "little soul" that could be trapped by an obeah man, he nodded. Zora Neale Hurston, in Haiti, once observed the dead rendering up its little soul: "The body of the dead man sat up with its staring eyes, bowed its head and fell back again . . . the loa or mystère which had lived in the dead man and controlled him was separated from him. He could go peacefully to rest and the loa would be employed by someone else."

Sometimes the soul departs from the body just before death. "This also happens," Mackie said, "when we dream; we leave our body and go elsewhere." Dreams are woven of the places the soul travels to when we are asleep. This departure of the soul before the occurrence of death is expressed by poet Sam Cornish:

"Before she died," said my grandmother, talking about her mother, "a giant bird flew into the room. He never left the room, and no one could ever find him in the room."

The dream of life turning into wings is expressed in the many Methodist and Baptist spirituals of African America, from "Fly, Fly Away" to "Dry Bones," both of which express physical and material release from the coils of life, the burdens that have been placed upon the weary.

Don't you hear the angel call?
Yes, I hear the angel call
I got the witness in my heart
And the glory in my soul.

Again, the witness is of the earth, alive, proud to be witnessing; and it is the heart, glad to be beating. But it is the soul, whose passage is reserved for glory, that experiences complete spiritual freedom.

In such readiness for "glory" the people sing out, eyes closed to the life they live, the air they breathe, for they know that this life is all bones, dry, dry bones "laid down in the valley" where "you can hear the word of the Lord." But the soul, now the soul goes upward, winged; it knows its home is over Zion's hill in the place where Jesus is Captain. The soul, they say, longs for a starry crown, for a cloudy robe; it longs to be free of its bodily burden, its woeful weight of bones.

All this imagery stems, directly or indirectly, from ancient days. In Egypt as well as sub-Saharan Africa, we find the image of the egg (life) floating above the mummy (death). Together, the two are a symbol of what awaits us in rebirth. The *egg,* is, therefore, a metaphor of the body, out of which the soul will emerge and rise after this transitory existence. To go out of Egypt, in revival church terms, means to be lifted out of bondage. But it also means to abandon the material world and to attain the Promised Land; to go metaphorically speaking, across the Red Sea and over the desert—from travail to transcendence. That blessings *await* the soul is a matter for religion and theology. That the soul *is* its own living blessing, here and now, is the realm of the natural mystic.

TRACK

Track-laying and track-laying men are legendary in the folk music of black America. We see, in verse, the silver rail in sunlight and starlight. And we hear, in song, the drawn-breath and the swing of the nine-pound hammer, held aloft and brought down with the high ring of iron on steel. Behind this lead music come the interstitial chants of the toiling chorus, track-layers all, singing songs to punctuate and accentuate their work, bodies flashing sweat as they enter the tunnel of the Chesapeake and Ohio Railway Company, the flare of lard oil and blackstrap dancing on rough rock walls.

It was in such a place, and on such an occasion, that the famous steel-driving man John Henry rose to the challenge of competing against a steam drill. Here, etched in song, is the legend of a black David set against an industrial-age Goliath. John Henry had, according to myth, two ten-pound hammers, though some claim he carried two twenty-pounders.

John Henry on the left; steam drill on the right. And the match was on.

The effort of this supreme contest—man against machine—was less a myth than a real life event. John Henry was an actual man. Some say he was black, others say yellow. A few report he was a wanted man, but most insist he was a family man, doing the best he could. But, in any case, he was a steel driver through and through, and whether he came from Jamaica, as rumors attest, or from Tallega, Kentucky, the story is the same:

Portrait of John Henry. Drawing by Devon Himes, Kansas City Art Institute.

The men that made that steam drill
Thought it was mighty fine.
John Henry sunk a fourteen-foot hole
And the steam drill only made nine.

Prison Yard. From the Collections
of the Library of Congress.

Whatever the various verses of the song, the outcome was in
favor of man over machine. The odds were against him, but John
Henry, the family man, won. Who knows, though, whether the
actual man survived the encounter, for in many versions of the
song, John Henry died of a "broken heart."

When John Henry was a little boy,
He was sitting on his mama's knee,
Says, "The Big Bend Tunnel on the C & O Road

Going to be the death of me, Lord, Lord
Going to be the death of me."

In railroad songs one finds a special kind of sweetness. This is because they were led, in the days of laying track, by a tremlo-voiced tenor whose job was to sing so soothingly that the men would not be hurt on the job. Unloading steel rails from flat cars and laying track on a roadbed was the hardest kind of work—a ninety-pound rail, thirty feet long, had to be lifted up and off, and down in perfect synchronicity, so that no broken bones accompanied its being set into place. The foreman sang out, "Now get around here, boys, and grab that rail like a cat grabbing a hot hoe-cake." They were to bow down and put glad hands upon it, raise it up, throw it away, and listen to it ring.

The spike-driving hammers rang their own special song, and as the track men stood on the rock where Moses stood, the hammer came down and the clock struck nine. There was gravel-dumping and tie-tamping and, all the while, high- and low-voice singing. And track songs, like all black American work songs, came from Africa and had the spirit of gathering and threshing, carding and spinning, harvesting and singing. It came from a long way away; from the immemorial time track of myth.

TRICKSTER

The gods of West Africa who came in dream and drum, in vision and remembrance to America were as varied as the people who brought them. Warriors, priests, farmers, and fishermen all had their gods; men and women of the Gold, Ivory, and Grain coasts; people of Gorée and Gambia, the Bights of Benin and Biafra—all had their gods.

Who were they, these beneficent and maleficent powers that inhabited everything from deep blue wells to the amber eye of a cat? There were river spirits and thunder gods, deities of snake lightning and serpent rainbow.

In addition to the multifarious deities, the gods and spirits that inhabited the West African cosmos, there were two other forces that every African brought with him to America and the West Indies. One of these was Fate and the other was Trickster. As black writer James Haskins has said:

West Africans believed that Fate ruled the universe. The destiny of each man, everything that happened in his life, was already worked out in a plan. Many Europeans believed in Fate too, but Europeans believed there was no way to escape the plan Fate had for them. Africans did believe there was a way out—through the divine trickster.

Accordingly, as Haskins points out, the trickster was neither a god nor a specific personage—it was a concept. For instance, the

Facing page: Anansi, The Spider Trickster. Art and photograph by Bobbe Besold.

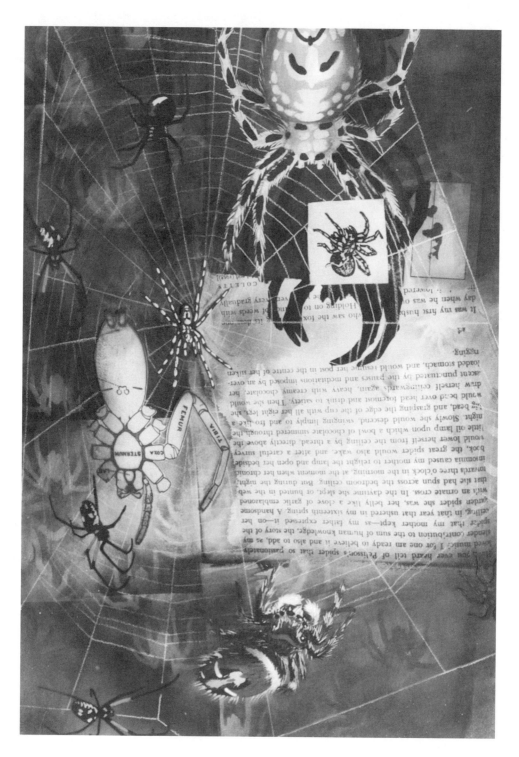

trickster might be a messenger of a god in the form of the deity's youngest child. The news thus brought to a man or his family, though it might be bad, could, if the trickster agreed, be changed.

Legba, the African god of gateways, houses, and shrines, became, in time, a trickster. As messenger of the gods, he had the power to set things up or down, come out well or come to naught—to make bad fates good and good fates bad; or to make into one a little bit of the other.

Anansi, the African spider trickster, splintered into many minor African-American deities when he arrived in the New World. He became, for example, the famous rascally rabbit and tricky hare of Uncle Remus. In the West Indies, he may have turned around and incorporated himself into a man of uncommon power, whom some islanders call Uncle Time, the one with "a peculiar smile, which can turn dark as sorrow or light as joy. His voice is soft as the bamboo leaf bowing in the breeze. His humor is dry as donkey tobacco, and, often, just as bitter. He seems to be all things to all people. And only those who have been deprived of him know the loss."

How the spider god turned readily from rabbit to man, and from man to the abstract concept of time, is sometimes explained by the genesis of African-American storytelling. Joel Chandler Harris, the author of the Uncle Remus stories, believed that many Creek Indian tales similar to his own had been borrowed from black people. But he was also aware of the alternative theory, cited by J. W. Powell of the Smithsonian, that the slaves had obtained their versions from the Indians. The great folklorist James Mooney observed that many Cherokee myths resembled Uncle Remus tales, and he resolved to prove the stories were of Native American origin.

A recent interpretation of this phenomenon is that of by fantasy master Roger Zelazny. He points out that—unlikely as it may seem—the Tar Baby tale originally came from India and was, in fact, a story of the Buddha and his classic battle with a "mud monster." Along the devious trade routes of slavery this story changed hands until East Indian, African, and American Indian influences had penetrated it and created an interchange that was ultimately American. So what happens when a rabbit loses his temper and does battle with a child of tar—all prearranged by a crafty fox—becomes a well-known tale, humorous, mainly, because the smart rabbit does not know his adversary is a lifeless lump. Lost in the translation, of course, is the notion, at least in part Native American, that mud and tar come from the earth, and that Earth is preeminently alive.

The line between American Indian and African-American tricksters becomes even more blurred when we consider that the rabbit hero-god was a universal tribal wonder-worker from the vast space of the Hudson Bay to the Gulf of Mississippi. Brer Rabbit, then, is none other than the Algonquian Great Hare. Yet it is also true that the principal trickster figure of East Africa is also the hare, who, in West Africa, was the shape-changer, Anansi.

Perhaps the drawing of the line between East and West and Here and There is an obsession that begs the issue and misses the point. Trickster, whether Indian, African, or American Indian, belongs to us all, the common heritage of human beings who learn from their betters; who, as Fate has decreed, happen to be animals rather than men.

TRINITY

Where there is faith
there is love
Where there is love
there is peace
Where there is peace
there is God
Where there is God
there is no need.
—*KELVIN RODRIQUES*

We were standing on the deck of a ship in the early morning, heading for the harbor of Port of Spain. Along with our friend, Malcolm, a Trinidadian, we were gathered at the rail, staring intently at the verdant mountains that are the promontories of the island. The Northern Range, running east to west, red-embered from the blossoming flamboyant trees, was, otherwise, a cool pastiche of muted blues and greens. Soon we would come round the Boca, the sea-mouth, and be greeted there by the eternal smells of the typical Caribbean port, the elixir of mixtures: scent of sour rum and burnt coffee, dead fish, fresh fruit, smoking trash, rubbery and oily fire-smells, and woven into all of this, the unspoiled redolence of African trees spawned so long ago in the great tidal pull of the continental drift.

Malcolm leaned into this breeze of mixed beauty, and pointed

The Holy Trinity of Ras Tafari.
Drawing by Mariah Fox.

to the three mountains that seemed to guard the bay. "Those three"—he smiled—"have been with me since childhood."

He nodded in the direction of the three mountains.

"Is that why they call it Trinidad?"

"Yes," he answered. "Clearly, those were the shepherds of Columbus; and many navigators since. They watch over the harbor, our protectors."

"Have you ever wondered, *why three*? Why there are always three wishes, three wisemen, three this, three that?"

Malcolm grinned. "You really don't know why three's so important?"

We said we did not.

"Three, where I come from, can mean many things. It could mean life, death, afterlife; or Father, Son, Holy Ghost. It could mean morning, noon, and night; mother, father, and child—oh, it could be so many things. . . ."

His smile now spilled graciously into laughter.

"You see," he remarked, "there are plenty of threes to go around. We like them and that's why we use them. I am thinking now of the African colors—red, gold, and green. These are the colors that control the earth—you know, every stoplight is red, gold, and green."

We had to laugh, for what he said was true. The three mountains, as we neared our destination, began to melt, the way large things change shape when you draw up to them.

"The mountains are gone."

"No, mon," Malcolm answered. "They are still three mountains, and they always will be; it is just that they have joined together as one, like Ham, Shem, and Japhet, Noah's three sons.

"Oh, in the islands," he went on, "we are still very much with our Bible. You see, those three sons of Noah's—Ham was African, Japhet was European, and Shem was Asian. People might say that one was 'black,' one 'white,' and one 'yellow,' but that is foolishness."

He shook his head in disapproval. Momentarily his face grew stern; then the smile came back, flashing, like the sun appearing from behind the clouds.

He touched us on the shoulder. "Do you know why I am saying that it is foolishness? Because color, per se, is foolish. There is no such thing as the white race; I mean, the 'white' race of people, or any race of color. We are all people with red blood, that is all. So, here it is, the three once again. Until the three sons of Noah recognize one another as true brothers, there will be no peace. No peace on earth at all."

TURTLE

Some fishermen had caught a great sea turtle on the north coast of Jamaica. We were watching them hand it up the beach—six grown men struggling—when an old man slipped out of the sea grape leaves, and knelt alongside us.

"To kill dat turtle is a sin," he said softly.

"Why?"

"Because dat animal is *we.*"

His eyes were filled with sadness as he said this. Together, we watched the villagers haul the huge creature along on its back. It made deep furrows in the sand with the ridge of its shell.

"The turtle is us?"

He nodded. "Our life, mon. We a-come from de same place of origin. Dey trow we—dem old pirate—in de hull of de merchant ship dem . . . and drag we ass all across de sea."

Sighing, he looked thoughtfully out toward the ocean, toward Haiti and beyond. "Yes, mon, four hundred years," he whispered. Then he told us the following tale, to which we have done nothing except to take it out of patois and place the words in common English.

I live on the sea. Like my father before me, and his father before him. I sleep when the water is calm; I swim in a dream. Overhead, the stars, and, in the morning, the sun dancing on the sea bottom.

We live on the sea. For there are many of us, and we travel together, hunting and gathering and living the way we have always lived. I know some of the old songs of when the earth was young; my people sing them and I know them from when I was little, and when I forget the words, I just lie back and listen to my mother sing; she sings in the old voice, whispery like the chant of the sea on the roof of the reef.

Morning comes when it is necessary to move. We leave our good hunting ground and travel afar. My father goes out, afloat, ahead of the others. He is the strongest paddler; no one can keep up with him. I watch the sun rise over his shoulder as he goes out. There is far-off thunder. My mother says the interlopers have come again, and the thunder belongs to them and to their boats.

After my father has gone way out ahead of us, my mother grows sad and afraid. We hear the sounds of the interlopers: metal noises, sparks of steel drowning in sea water, bad-tasting bubbles of death breathing out into our world. This we have tasted before. It is all right, we are used to it. But still, I fear for my father. He is so far out. The sea is flat before my eye, crinkling merrily in the sun, the sun.

We paddle and row, all of us—the old and young alike. No one rests when there is the threat of danger on the water. And the interlopers make darkness come to pass. We do nothing to them, for we keep to ourselves. We like the light and the dazzle of the sea and the deep gray-green beds of grass where we hunt to feed our families.

We give our bodies to the seasons of the water, but we capture no one, we hurt no one. Once, I saw my father attack an interloper. He wrestled with him and cut him, slashing him fatally. I saw then, as the interloper lay spread-eagled and dead in the water, that his blood was red like mine, like all of ours. And I wondered why we weren't the same. . . .

Morning has come and gone. The gleaming ruins of antler corals are sunless now and the eelgrass sleeps, flowing dreamily this way and that, one side then another. And now, the eel snakes of the sea come out; they twine like vines about the bone-white staghorns, look lifeless, and await the unwary fish. I have eaten; my belly is full. My father has not returned and my mother is worried. We are becalmed, the windward shroud lies motionless, and we with it, dreamy as a driftwood log.

Facing page: Sea Turtle Skull and Turtle Motif. Art and photograph by Bobbe Besold.

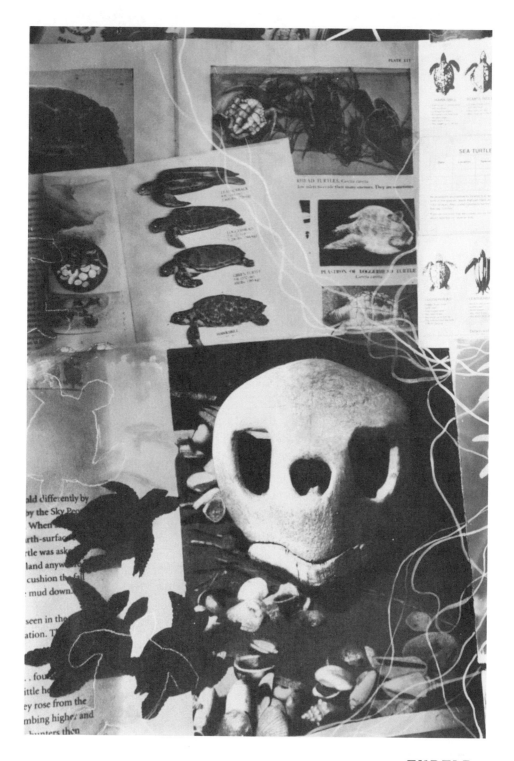

I want to sleep, my eyelids are heavy, but my mother is so worried, I cannot. We wait, afloat. The turtle moon comes up and over the vault of heaven. We sigh.

And wait.

Shortly before dawn, my mother wakes me. I hear metal movements, rudders cranking, squealing of reels, a pulling of pulleys.

Voices in the distant sea calm come to our ears.

Interlopers, shouting, singing. Metal-voiced, monotonous songs, not pretty like the songs of the old ones who remember the First Earth.

Voices. Far off.

"Get him in the boat."

The first voice of grated steel.

"Let's lash him, tie him good."

The second voice, as alien as the first.

We listen; the voices travel long and lonely upon the sea, adream in calm.

We swim out. I paddle with my mother; she is stronger, her strokes hard and sure and deep-delved. Her arms work without tiring, but soon I am tired and must rest.

The voices are closer now.

Gliding over the crystal beds of night-blooming anemones, soundless as spirits, just the dip-dipping of our moon-pearled paddles.

Dawn is drawing nigh. Soon the sea will again spark to life and diamond the decks of many a boat. But my father—alas, I know this, I know it well—is in jail. The interlopers have picked him up.

I do not really understand their speech, but it comes to me clearly who they are from the way they speak. We speak a different language; the sea is in what we say, the sway of the sea-drift. The twirl of the tines of the littlest wavelet is in our words; while the interlopers speak a jargon of steel moods and iron recollections.

Beyond tired, I am paddling now in a dream. I know I will see my father soon, perhaps for the last time. My mother paddles ever on, her strong arms agleam, fringed in the blue fire of the moon.

The approach of something; a large boat looms in the water. I see the prison yard, the cells of gloom. My father is there, strapped and roped. He cannot move, yet he sings. There are others; some chained, some weighted with timbers so they cannot move. Most are on their backs, arms out, bellies exposed. It is hard to sing like that, yet I hear my father's song turn in the red-rising sun.

The moonglow filters out of the incandescent air; the sunglow emerges, a starfish, golden-rayed, touching every corner of the sea.

We arrive just as he is taken away on the prison boat. We have been paddling all night, and even my powerful mother cannot push forth any longer.

The water has changed from silver to gold to green and blue. We wait, breathing hard. A spice wind, laced with earth smells, dries our nostrils. Hot sun, soft wind; father going away, singing.

The song he sings I have heard before. It is of the turtle moon.

"I live on the sea," he sings as the interlopers take him away in their prison boat. "As my father before me, and his father before him. I sleep when the water is calm; I swim in a dream . . ."

That is the last I can make out of his song as the boat goes away, belching black oil in its white wake.

On the way back, I ask my mother the same question we have been asking since the beginning of the earth and the spooling of the spellbound sea. "Why," I question as we tiredly paddle home, "why do the interlopers hate us?"

And my mother replies: "We are free, my son, and they are not."

"But now Father isn't free anymore," I say.

"Your father," she answers sternly, "will always remain free. He is of the First Earth, a Turtle Person."

As we paddle through the golden dawn, I wonder if any of the interlopers know that my father is twice two hundred years.

UNCLE TIME

Uncle Time is good and bad,
young and old, creepy and cranky,
spotless and handsome.
He is the keeper of the gate
and the child messenger of the gods.
He is a spiderman, cunning;
a web-spinner, funning.
Nobody laughs like Uncle Time.
And nobody misses him
but those deprived of him.
—*GERALD HAUSMAN & KELVIN RODRIQUES*

Uncle Time was a small dark West Indian man. No one knew
where he lived, or where he had come from, but around him there
grew a tangled wreath of legends, a mist of truths and half-truths
and some outright lies. Rumor seemed to follow him wherever he
went. Someone said that he'd killed a man, done some time in jail
at Richmond Farm, over by Highgate. But no one knew for sure.

One day Uncle Time appeared on the road between Castle
Gordon and Port Maria. At the double bend in the road there was
a Leyland truck, a huge diesel hauling gravel from the Wog Water
stone pit.

And there was that small dark West Indian man, Uncle Time.
He was walking along, seemingly unaware of the truck, but he
was also directly in its path.

The big truck was bearing down.

The little man, in sight of the truck, made no move to get out of the way.

The horn blasted like a wounded bull.

The chrome grille of the diesel grinned murderously in the sun.

Seconds before collision, the little man leaped up—and landed on the roof of the truck. He'd sailed twelve feet through the air and alighted like a butterfly, unhurt. And it was as if it had never happened.

Legends like this spread all over Castle Gordon, and into the hills of St. Mary. The townspeople dubbed their subject Uncle Time. They compared him to Anansi, the magic spider-man of Africa, the superhero whom no being—mortal or immortal—could kill.

One day a Chinese man named Chin was carrying a load of cane down Grant's Town hill. As it happened, he passed Uncle Time on the narrow goat trail by Blue Harbour. But when he turned to see if it was really Uncle Time, Chin saw only his own shadow. Where had the little man gone? He looked into a tree and saw Uncle Time reclining upon a limb, eating a Bombay mango.

Then there was the boy named Percy, who had failed the Common Entrance Exam. He suffered such shame, this boy, that he planned to hang himself. And he went into the bush to do so. But once he got there, and had readied his noose for the big swing into eternity, who should he see but Uncle Time?

Uncle Time, was watching the whole thing and smiling. He offered Percy some bananas from the bunch he'd just picked, and told him to stick around and he might see something. They sat on the limb of a big guango tree, eating bananas and tossing the peels to the ground.

Presently, there appeared an old beggar man, so ragged and toothless that he couldn't care for himself any longer. The grimy beggar man, spying the pile of banana skins, fell upon them like a starved dog, and, growling, began to devour them. Percy, seeing someone far more unfortunate than himself, realized that his own situation was not so bad. At least he was well fed. Thus he vowed never to try and take his own life again.

Background and facing page: Mr. Denzel at Blue Harbour, Jamaica. Photograph by Hannah Hausman.

Once there was a fisherman named Milo. Milo used to go so far out to sea chasing tuna that he often fell asleep in his boat and woke up the next morning off the coast of Cuba. One time when he was on one of these distant sea journeys, he saw something that looked like a turtle, rising and settling in the waves.

He knew that it was very late in the day because when he left port, the sun was on the left side of his chest. Now, heading home, the sun was warming the back of his right shoulder. That was how he knew where he was. Still, he was several miles out to sea when he saw this bobbing thing, rising and falling in the deep blue troughs.

Perhaps it is a turtle, he thought.

Then, he was close to it. What a surprise: The mysterious presence on the high seas was none other than Uncle Time, who explained that he was "just out for a swim."

Milo was amazed to see that Uncle Time, though he accepted a ride to shore, was not afraid of sharks, nor even of drowning.

"You could die out here," Milo said, giving the small man his hand and pulling him in.

However, Uncle Time merely smiled and took a seat in the stern of the boat.

"Have you no fear?" Milo asked.

Uncle Time smiled, and said nothing.

"A storm could come up and drown you!" Milo threatened.

Uncle Time said nothing.

For a while, it seemed that everyone in the town of Castle Gordon had a story about Uncle Time. Wherever he went, something extraordinary seemed to happen. He was, the people felt, a man of greatness. Yet many of the things he did were common, and often passed unnoticed.

Now, as it happened, there came a night when some thieves were parceling out the spoils of a robbery. They'd taken refuge under the limbs of a wild fig tree, the roots of which went deep into the ground. It was a good place not to be seen, and the three men were passing crumpled bills when a hundred-dollar note dropped into one of the caves made by the roots of the wild fig.

"Lower yourself down dere, mon, and fetch me dat note," the leader said to one of his men.

"It too dark fe see," the man said, cringing in the shadows.

"Tek the flashlight down into de cave, mon, and carry the note up back."

Without further argument, the man slid down the fig root into the black cave.

"Fetch the note up back, mon," the leader shouted impatiently.

Now the man saw the note lying open before his eyes, but he also heard something in the cave that stopped him in his tracks.

"A ting growl down here," the man quavered.

He slid up the cabled root, just as the growls grew louder. All three men heard them by then.

"Run," the leader yelled, "it's a duppy!"

The next morning the stolen money turned up on the doorstep of Miss June Chung, owner of Chung's Grocery in Port Maria. It was her store that had been robbed. All the money was returned, or most of it anyway.

"Me see him wid me own eye," one of the thieves, who was drinking at a rum shop, said later that night.

"What you see, mon? Stop your bawling and tell us—"

"Uncle Time."

After that, legends stretched out like a mystical web and covered the town. There was the tale of the burning mongoose . . . the tale of the beating heart in the paper bag . . . the tale of the rat bat with the bammy cake in its mouth. . . .

And all of these tales were somehow imputed to Uncle Time. Whatever happened, for a while, was his doing. Be the matter normal or abnormal, Uncle Time was the unmoved mover, the thing around which all other things revolved. And yet, as the

rumor mill ground out rumors, the people saw less and less of that little dark West Indian man.

Then word had it that Uncle Time was living in the ruins of an old great house, a slave plantation, outside Castle Gordon. The ruined house was surrounded by a ghostly garden of neglected flowers and trees. No one went there, for the place was crawling with duppies.

Now, as soon as it became known that Uncle Time was staying there, the three thieves decided to pay him a visit. They came, one night, well armed with pistols and machetes.

"All right," the leader said. "You do what me se fe do, seen?"

The other two nodded, and answered, "Seen."

The plan seemed simple enough. They rounded the big breadfruit tree that sheltered the overgrown yard, and saw the little dark man around whom so many legends of magic deeds had spun.

Uncle Time was squatting before a fire of pimento sticks, roasting a yam for his supper.

"Look pon him now," the leader scoffed, "him just a likkle mon." He spat on the ground, walked boldly into the firelight. The others, doglike, trailed behind.

The leader then strode up to Uncle Time, unholstered his revolver, and emptied it into him.

The pistol shots shattered the still air, sending squeaking, flapping rat bats up into the night sky.

Uncle Time was lying on the ground.

The leader cried out, "Him dead, me kill Uncle Time!"

First one thief, then the other stepped into the circle of fire. What they saw made them feel queasy. The little man was lying on his side with his eyes tightly closed. They couldn't have explained why, but the sight made them ill.

"Chop him!" the leader commanded.

The two men made no movement.

"Chop him!" he screamed.

Then something strange happened.

From out of the quivering trees came cords of silk. The thieves felt them bind their heads and shoulders, their arms and ankles, and though they struggled to get free, their bodies were soon sealed with silken bonds as strong as steel.

The thieves were bound from head to foot; and the silk fell from the sky, and turned them into cocoons of snow.

Mummified, they remained.

Frozen in place.

This is how the townspeople of Castle Gordon found the three thieves the following morning. And if you ask someone in Castle Gordon what happened to those men, he or she will point to the nearest tree, and show you the magic web of Anansi, breathing sweetly in the sunlight, bowing in the wind.

So that is all there is to say of the three thieves.

Of Uncle Time, however, more can always be said.

You may see him on sunny days and gloomy days, sitting under his favorite palm tree over by Pagee Beach. Or up on the peninsula, by Black Sand. He has nowhere to go and nothing to do. But he is always around, and people are always talking about him, saying this, that, and the other.

Somehow, you can usually find people gathered around, making idle remarks about how he lives, and what life would be like without him. But, no matter what they say about him, the people know, now and forever more, that you can't kill Uncle Time.

Nor can you make a fool out of Anansi.

UNDERGROUND RAILROAD

It had no tracks, no engine of iron and steam, no carriages of steel and wood. But it had a destination; the Promised Land. And of the four million African-American slaves who dreamed of passage upon its invisible rails, only a small number—probably somewhere between thirty thousand and a hundred thousand—fled from bondage. Their tales of the suffering and privation they endured while making their way to freedom would fill as many books.

Some traveled ingeniously, like Henry Brown, who mailed himself in a box "with a few biscuits and a bladder of water." But most took to the track on foot, following the North Star alone. Defying slave hunters and slave laws, runaways left with their lives ever on the line. Truly, they were not safe anywhere in the nation.

John Brown, warrior and martyr, once led eleven slaves in the dead of winter along the Underground Railroad. A thousand miles they journeyed, facing all kinds of obstacles, from Missouri to Ontario. What signs, you may ask, aside from the icy glitter of the North Star, told them that they were, in fact, on the right track? On one lawn, the story is told, there was a statue of a black groomsman whose hand held a flag of welcome if the owner of the house, a federal judge, was not at home. His wife was an agent of the Underground Railroad, who worked in secret underneath her own roof and under the watchful eyes of her own husband.

In some places, whole towns were on the Underground Line; in

Harriet Tubman. Drawing by Brian Byrd, Kansas City Art Institute.

others it crisscrossed and looped through the house of yes and around the house of no. Like fireflies the lights winked on, went out, said come, said stay. Barns, churches, houses, and always the starlit fields of lop-eared corn, the burnt stubble of winter-blasted stalks. Here, a man stuffed his coat full of turkey feathers for insulation and protection, and no matter how many times he was seen and shot at, he somehow managed to live. There, a whole family hid in the hold of a Mississippi steamboat. Here, secret signs—passwords and handshakes—gave a man hope as he huddled in a farmer's wagon. There, a woman wore out her shoes, but not her welcome in a dark summer cellar, watched over by a child of mercy.

Indian Territory in Oklahoma was a stopping-off place, and sometimes a home, for slaves. Today their descendants are known as Seminole freedmen or black Seminoles. African-American writer Charles L. Blockson has written: "In Spanish Florida, blacks had lived in their own villages, paying tribute to the chiefs and fighting beside them against American intruders. By speaking English and interpreting white ways, many became influential in tribal affairs. When the Seminoles were evicted to Indian Territory, some five hundred blacks went along."

There were, of course, false stops along the Underground Railroad. These, like Venus flytraps, beckoned sweetly to trap the unsuspecting. In such perilous country, where friend and foe wore the same apparently trustworthy smile and where wolves in sheep's clothing opened doors and lit fires of friendliness, fugitives had nothing to depend on but their own heart and luck: stay and die, go and live. The only safety was the night, the North Star burning, the foot still free, the mind yet alert. But the dream of freedom was as distant as the Big Dipper, and when Harriet Tubman crossed the slender suspension bridge over the Niagara River into Ontario, who better than she knew the mystic phrase "Follow the drinking gourd"? On the Underground Railroad, there was no guarantee except to keep walking, crossing, praying, and believing that John Brown's body was not—nor would it be—a-moldering in the grave.

VAUDOU

The distinction between secular and sacred, natural and supernatural, religion and magic darkens and disappears when one speaks of vaudou. Spelled variously, the word we have come to know as "voodoo" is the name of a cult, a religion, a system of thought whose African roots are undeniably deep and tangled. In general, it has been cast in most Western writing as a religion of sacrifice, a satanic and collective burst of blood, in which pagan gods are honored with drums, dance, and spirit possession.

What is the truth; and what, precisely, is vaudou?

According to black writer James Haskins, "The word *vodun* comes from the West African Ewe tribe and is derived from *vo* (apart), which can be interpreted to mean *set apart* or *holy*."

Other writers have accurately described voodoo as a religious belief carried into action through ritual—through dancing, drumming, and singing. In the act of dance, the participant becomes entranced, and is thus "mounted" by a god or *loa*, whose influence—usually benign—completely alters the individual's consciousness. The resultant state, beyond intoxication and exultancy, is a fusion of man and god, a joining, a mounting of the all-powerful and the earthly, the divine and the mortal. For this reason, many writers have described voodoo, not in African terms, but according to Greek mythology, speaking of Apollo's winged feet, Hercules' great strength momentarily visiting and briefly loaned to a human being. Examples are also cited in the antics of the ancient Greek Bacchanal, the so-called celebration of wine, women, and song. Further distractions of this sort have been imposed on voodoo in the form of, unlikely as it may sound in this context, Catholicism. But, in the words of Zora Neale Hurston, "and right here, let it be said that the Haitian gods, mystères, or Loa are not the Catholic calendar of saints done over in black as has been stated by casual observers."

The gods of Africa, entrusted to memory, underwent a sea change in crossing the Atlantic. What was lost was not destroyed, but altered. In the milieu of master and slave, the old gods took on new meaning, new power. The Candomble of Brazil, the Santería of Cuba, the Shango of Trinidad, and the vaudou of Haiti (and New Orleans) took on a great New World vitality. Far from lost, the gods grew in stature, became more familiar than ever. And as necessity dictated, the enslaved became, in the mystical sense of the word, empowered.

From the beginning, vaudou was a mystical cult that gave its believers a power over the utter desolation of slavery. In the islands generally, and Haiti in particular, the slave, by conjoining himself with the mystery of vaudou, enhanced his ability to overcome his helplessness. The islands, in contrast to the North American continent, presented the slave with an Africa-like landscape into which, if he escaped successfully, he might never return to the horrors of slavery. Vaudou was often the religion of the runaway, the Maroon, the fugitive slave. In jungle and mountain retreats, the drum and the dance reasserted themselves and vaudou rites gave antiwhite resistance a definite methodology.

During the late 1790s Haitian rebels such as Jean François, who filled his tent with cats of many colors; Mackandal, who spread vaudou and poison, killing blacks and whites alike; Boukman, whose followers drank the blood of a black hog; and Toussaint Louverture, the bush doctor who drove Napoleon's army into the sea and truly liberated Haiti—all of these vaudou resistance fighters used the hypnotic religion of ancient Africa to further their cause and bring an end to slavery. Interestingly enough, in the Americas, vaudou reached white, as well as primarily black, fol-

lowers. Although voodooism, as it was called, was once officially
banned, it existed in Georgia, South Carolina, and Louisiana.
"Refugee French planters, their slaves and black freedmen who
had escaped from the slave revolution in Haiti and Santo Domin-
go," Haskins reports, "found their way to New Orleans with the
result that some ten thousand people, white and black, rekindled
the flame of vaudou." In spite of ordinances against it, voodooism
thrived and Congo Square of a Sunday resounded with drums.
Almost from the very moment of importation, vaudou formed an
audience in America that was both rural and urban, black and
white, wealthy and poor; that audience has existed from roughly
1800 until the present.

We may never know the names of the magical presences, the
mystères of the vaudou pantheon, in their entirety because, as the
old was grafted onto the new, places and forces reshaped both
gods and demigods, not to mention the endless variations of

*The Vaudou Meeting in the Old
Brick-yard.* From the Collections
of the Library of Congress.

ancestors whose powers were only locally known. Zora Neale Hurston has written that in Haiti, "it is agreed that there are two *classes* of deities, the Rada or Arada and the Petro. The Rada gods are the 'good' gods and are said to have originated in Dahomey. The Petro gods are the ones who do evil work and are said to have been brought over from the Congo." A Rada deity of supreme significance is Damballah. His symbol is the serpent and he is, therefore, often identified with Moses, whose rod, Hurston tells us, "is said to have been a subtle serpent." Damballah has also been compared to St. Patrick (whose image is depicted with snakes). In any case, Damballah's grace and specific power arises from the serpent-staff; like that of Moses and Aaron, his magic is biblically good, and never, they say, capricious or bad. Papa Damballah, he is called, representative of the source of life, the Serpent, who, also in Native American belief, is the rainbow, the white god, the joiner of heaven and earth. In vaudou, Papa Damballah guards domestic bliss and is a dualized deity, a bi-sexual concept of the Creator—once again revealing the subtle nature of the ever-elusive mythical serpent.

The female counterpart of Papa Damballah is Erzulie Frieda. She is, however, husbandless; or, to put it another way, her husband is all men, though none in particular. She is, above all, the pure and perfect image of woman, and as the reflection of Damballah, her will is cast in dreams and hearts. No mortal woman can compare to her; nor would she attempt to do so. Men in Haiti devote themselves to her in a formal religious service that is sacred, and not in any way profane. As Hurston has observed, "Every Thursday and every Saturday, millions of candles are lighted in her honor." Although Erzulie is comparable to the Virgin Mary, she is neither passive nor chaste; her perfection is that she offers herself to mortal man, a goddess whom all men aspire to meet. The jealousy of Erzulie is such that women fear her wrath and merely offer their spiritual rival mute acceptance. A man, however, who does not respond in dream to Erzulie's whispers and silken offerings, may be visited by extreme bad luck. His consequent—and penitent—obeisance is a vaudou ceremony wherein Erzulie is properly placated.

Another aspect of Erzulie Frieda's countenance, a Rada deity, is an old woman, a witch whose eyes are reddened; she is Erzulie the Red-Eyed, a kind of flip side to the beautiful amorous goddess Erzulie, whose gold chain and ring and perfect female attributes make her a personification of sexual love.

Above and beyond the religious significance of vaudou, there is, and always has been, an intensely political overtone to the cult. Forged out of the spirit of rebellion, vaudou still has no political rival in Haiti, except perhaps the disease of AIDS; and yet as a political tool, it has been abused over the centuries by one mono-maniacal despot after another. In Haiti, as Amy Wilentz observes, "Voodoo simply upheld whatever system was in place, and, even in the smallest of villages, that was usually a system of gross exploitation." However, the power of vaudou is such that even death in the form of AIDS is no match for it. For in dying there is the return to *ginen,* return to Africa, return to the very taproot of vaudou. The circle is complete, in life and in death; vaudou knows no greater force than itself—the serpent swallowing its tail. No wonder its presence still excites such gross fear and misunder-standing. As the ultimate slave religion, it was also the greatest weapon against slavery. When slavery goes, perhaps vaudou will go with it. And there is the snake with the head at both ends—who is the slave and who is the master?

WATER

In world folklore water is the element that restores the dead to life, cures illness, bestows immortality. Ancient Egyptians believed that water was a sacred purifier, not only in a superficial sense but in the transmission of divine grace. As primeval matter, it brought forth all things, awakened the heart, and was, generally, the element of feminine principle; yet it also had the power to father, as well as to mother, the human spirit; thus the tale of Nun and Naunet, who together formed an androgynous unity. In the festival of Osiris, a model phallus and a vase of water were carried at the head of the procession. As the god of vegetation, Osiris himself was regarded as the lord of the waters of the Nile, whereas Isis was metaphor for the fertile land.

African water myths are abundant and it is no coincidence that African slaves carried these to the New World. Water purification rites exist in the West Indies today much as they once did in Africa centuries ago. In fact, it was the use of water in the baptismal rite that helped make the Baptist church so popular with southern American and West Indian blacks.

What is water sign?

On one level it is merely the promise of rain, for which there are abundant cultural attitudes and stances, including ways of walking, standing, and sitting without talking. The following is from *Deep Like the Rivers: Stories of my Negro Friends* by Marcia Emmons.

When you're standing in your door and see the clouds begin to come up and the lightning go to flashing, and the thunder hitting right along behind it, you must just stand there and watch it, and don't say nothing. Then as the clouds get closer and the thunder claps right over your head, and a few drops of rain begin to fall, and the chickens begin to make it home, you just stand there and watch it, and don't say nothing...then it goes to just pouring down rain. You just set and watch it and don't say nothing...

Water falling from the sky is an occasion for ceremony or observance in African-American lore. A rainstorm, replete with flashes of fire, and which threatens to turn into something else, must be watched in reverence, in silence. For "the fire next time" could be this time. The folk song verse goes, "God gave Noah the rainbow sign/said it won't be water/but fire next time." Best, then, to sit in silence and meditate upon the power of heaven.

According to Zora Neale Hurston, the most awesome sight of water comes not from the sky, but from the earth: It is the famous Saut d'Eau waterfall in Haiti. She describes the thousands who come here to wash away their troubles, to cleanse themselves inside and out in the "leap of the water," which is the literal translation of the place name.

Once, as Hurston explains in *Tell My Horse,* "a beautiful luminous virgin lit the fronds of a palm tree there and waved her gorgeous wings and blessed the people." A sign of this magnitude had never been seen on this island, which is noted for its magical dispensations. After singing a beautiful song, the angelic presence disappeared; the people remained, however, worshiping the palm tree where the angel had presented herself.

In time the image of the Blessed Virgin became a vision shared by many people who had not even seen it, and thus the palm tree became a symbol of the holy event. As a result, the Catholic church, feeling a sense of abandonment, took action. Since the palm tree was the object of adoration, a priest, taking charge for the church, ordered the tree destroyed. When no one came for-

Background: Young Boys on the Okavango Delta, Africa. Photograph by Barbara Baumann.

ward to uphold his order, he himself struck the first blow with a machete. However, the blade bounced harmlessly off the tree and struck him a deadly blow on the head. After the priest died in Port-au-Prince, the church dealt more effectively with the tree, killing it and then building a chapel in its place. "Several churches have burned on that site," reported Hurston, "and one was destroyed by lightning."

It is no wonder the ancient Egyptians regarded water as the most sacred of symbols, for like the Pueblo people of North America, it brings forth the union of all the other elements: earth, air, and fire. And just as water liberated the dead, so it also warned the living that earth is not as stable as it appears. Fire must bow, too—along with Air—when Water raises her head and lets fall her curtain of hair.

Facing page: Sacred Waterfall, Haiti. The American Center of Haitian Art, Matlacha, Florida. Photograph by R. D. Johnson.

WEST

Knowledge of the historical legacy of African Americans in western America is full of error and misunderstanding. Scholarly neglect and racial distortion play a prominent role in the reason why the western frontier would appear to be a "red and white" tableau. In truth, blacks played a major part in the settling of the West; they were railroad workers, miners, farmers, cowboys, soldiers, and as recent evidence suggests, entrepreneurs.

What scholars are unearthing is that the myth of the Golden West, the land of O. Henry's Pimienta pancakes, full of bright promise in the pan, was as attractive to blacks as to whites, if not more so. Blacks, too, it would seem, followed the hackneyed advise "Go west, young man." Old, young, and in-between, go they did.

According to *U.S. News & World Report:*

A census of old California shows that by 1790, 18 percent of the population of the territory was African American. By 1890, 518,986 African Americans—about 4 percent of the nation's black populace—lived west of the Mississippi. Twenty-six of the original 44 settlers of the pueblo of La Nuestra Senora de los Angeles—the wellspring of modern-day Los Angeles—were black, as were many in the western fur trade from the 1820s to the 1840s. As many as one in four cowboys who participated in the cattle drives through Texas was African American.

The Sign Language. Drawing by
Fredering Remington. From the
Collections of the Library of Con-
gress.

What drove these already driven human beings to an unknown
and perhaps worse landscape than the one they had already
known? Well, maybe those who had been given a bellyful of Missouri, originally nicknamed the Puke State, and Kansas, first
called the Grasshopper State, came to California for the climate.
Everyone said there was a pot of gold at the end of God's rainbow,
and in the Bear State this proved not only figuratively but literally
true. California was said to have a climate so healthy that they
"had to shoot a man in order to start a graveyard." So the promise
of freedom, comfort, and immediate wealth had much to do with

the new western mythology in the minds of whites and blacks alike.

But perhaps of all the palpable lures given, African Americans saw with most interest the possibility of renewal in racially separatist settlements: More than sixty all-black towns sprang up between Alabama and California. It was hope as much as money that fueled the so-called exoduster movement of 1879-80.

"As was often the case during the settling of the West, black pioneers were promised fertile fields, abundant water, shady trees, and plenty of game. Instead, arriving blacks found that the best farmland surrounding the town was already taken by whites. There were no trees, and the game was scarce." (U.S. NEWS & WORLD REPORT)

However, in California, reality took a backseat to mythology. In 1851, just four years after the inception of the Gold Rush, the commissioner of patents in San Francisco announced that he had been presented with "an onion weighing 21 pounds, a turnip as big around as the top of a flour barrel, a cabbage measuring 13 feet, six inches around, a beet weighing 63 pounds, and carrots three feet in length." Such abundance must have impressed the African-American farmer more than the infamous promise of forty acres and a mule.

The subsequent disappointment, on finding a continent confounded with dust, delirium, wind storms, and lightning, was a biblical curse unto the eyes of many blacks. For, in just proportion to the lies of magnanimity were the twisted tales of sorrow; word got out that "hoppers ate all but the wagon sheet" or "everything but the mortgage." One exaggeration included the claim that there was a California grasshopper so big it ate a farmer's team of mules, then went on to pitch horseshoes for the wagon.

In spite of such scornful stories, however, some black towns prospered into yet a newer speculator's myth: true lies, actual prosperity. For instance, the Kansas town of Nicodemus, established in 1879 by a white land speculator and his black partner:

. . . eventually boomed into one of the models of black indepen-
dence in the West. It boasted a church, a post office, a hotel, a general
store and two black-run newspapers. Edward P. McCabe was elected
as Kansas's first black auditor general. Similarly, the all-black town
of Boley, founded in 1904 in Oklahoma and also landed as a model
of black separatist self-determination, had a black city council and
its own waterworks, electric power company, banks and stores. (U.S.
NEWS & WORLD REPORT)

What happened, eventually, to Nicodemus and Boley occurred
in many midwestern and western towns: Boom faded to bust, or
boom-fated-bust, as it were. As regional economies struggled for
survival, the same triumvirate—greed, graft, and grit—that
"made the West great" worked like the devil to level it. Nicodemus
lost a bid to have a railroad; Boley "fell prey to the demographic
shift to big cities." However, one suspects the legacy of racism here
as well; voting rights did not exist for blacks, neither were there
privileges for African-American millionaires. Black was black, and
that meant poor, regardless of finances.

And so, what of the accomplishments of the Buffalo Soldiers
and the black cowboys and even the hero mythos of such outlaws
as Railroad Bill, who rivaled Jesse James? They were shoved under
the carpet under the more important heading of "White Makes
Right." The West, the legend went, was golden; sun brown did not
mean sun black. In the end, even such romantic chroniclers of the
westward movement as Frederic Remington, who had, at first,
depicted blacks in his paintings, later left them out. And, as
recently as two years ago, the U.S. Postal Service, portraying rodeo
star Bill Pickett in its "Legends of the West" stamp series, mistakenly printed the portrait of the black cowboy's brother, Ben—a
true case of myth overtaking myth, and leaving truth behind. If
Bill had not invented bull-dogging, perhaps no one would have
really cared.

WORD

The Dogon of Mali and Burkina Faso view creation as having several stages, each culminating in a sacred word. The first of these is the sound of the grass (singing); the second is the sound of weaving; the third is the sound of grain (threshing) and of the drum. These sacred words, given by God, represent the beginning of humankind's psychic growth. Thus, in "the sound of grass," we embrace the earth, our mother. In weaving, we have the social integration of man and woman, and the larger community of the tribe. The word of the sacred granary is food; the drum is the medium of culture through which all share what is known.

The Dogon believe that when God made love to his earth-wife, water, the divine seed, entered the womb of the Earth Mother, and this resulted in the birth of twins. Their bodies, we are told in the myth, were snakelike, green, and sleek, shining like water and covered with short green hairs. The latter hint at the coming of vegetation and germination, and the twins are like the First People of the Native American Southwest. First Man and First Woman, to Pueblo and Navajo alike, are representative of corn, and are depicted as human-headed, leaf-armed, and rooted in the earth.

Relatives of the Dogon Hero Twins are common to most mythologies throughout the world. Their destiny sends them to Heaven, where they take instruction from their father: "Not that God had to teach them speech, that indispensable necessity of all beings." No, the pair were born complete with eight limbs, like the

Facing page: Scientifik. Photograph courtesy of Peter Bodtky

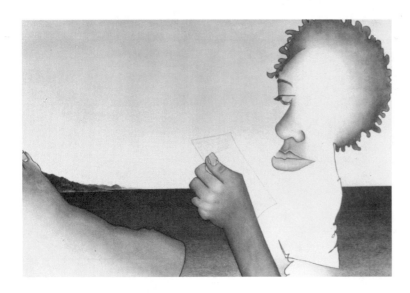

Dreaming the Word. Watercolor by Lisa Remeny. Tropic Arts, Coconut Grove, Florida.

eight-leaved ancestor, First Corn. The number eight is especially significant to the Dogon, for it is the symbolic number of speech. Conversely, it is also interesting to note that the Dogon do not believe the Earth Mother herself has speech, but rather is all-nurturing energy, the mother incarnate, possessed of all and by all possessed. She is, therefore, the divine incubator, and thus remains silent.

The Nummo, twin progeny of Mother Earth, are themselves a channel for moisture—they are intermediaries between earth and sun, the presence of which creates life-giving moisture.

What comes out of the twins' mouths when they speak? A warm vapor, they say, which itself constitutes speech. Vapor, as we know, is in essence water; all water may be said to "speak," to make sound. So it is that the *word* is life—without moisture, wetness, we die.

As a result of the Nummo's work on earth and as intermediaries with the sun, growth begins; in evolutionary terms, this is the greening of the planet. Symbolically, it may be expressed thus:

The coiled fringes of the skirt were therefore the chosen vehicle for the words which the Spirit desired to reveal to the earth . . . with magic power he put hands to lips while he plaited the skirt. The moisture of his words was imparted to the damp plaits. In these fibres full of water and words, placed over his mother's genitalia, Nummo is thus always present.

Thus clothed, the earth had language, the first language of this world.... Its syntax was elementary, its verbs few, and its vocabulary without elegance.... Such as it was, this ill-defined speech sufficed for the great works of the beginning of all things. (from The Mythology of All Races, *Vol. 7)*

Phrased differently, but with the same intent, is Psalm 104, in which the Lord's presence, his voice upon the land, puts moisture upon the earth:

Thou makest springs gush forth in the valleys; they flow between the hills, they give drink to every beast of the field; the wild asses quench their thirst, by them the birds of the air have their habitation; they sing among the branches. From Thy lofty abode Thou waterest the mountains; the earth is satisfied with the fruit of Thy work.

It is a short step, though some might call it a leap, from the Africa of the oldest continent on earth to the Africa of America, which may be imagined as the newest. From the dawn of time to—some say—the dusk of today. The word is with us, great within us. The creation is wet on the tongue of the poet of God, whether we find him, or her, on the street, in the pulpit, or in the performance hall.

When God first created the earth, they said the devil was loose down on earth, walking around and catching souls. He caught so many he had his both arms full, and one in his mouth. And he passed where a lady was washing, and she asked him, "Mr. Devil, are you coming back tomorrow?" And he says, "Yes." So he lost the soul he had in his mouth, and came back with only two. Then he

studied a plan to hold the soul that he carried in his mouth. He put a stick in his mouth, and had the little devil ask him, "Mr. Devil, are you coming back tomorrow?" And he practiced saying the word, "Mhm," When he went the next day, he caught three souls, and passed the lady washing again. And she asked him, "Mr. Devil, are you coming back tomorrow?" He said, "Mhm." So he saved that soul.

That's where the word Mhm *comes from.*

—FROM AMERICAN NEGRO FOLKTALES *BY RICHARD M. DORSON*

And what of the word that is the twin of "mhm"? The word "ah," a combination of satisfaction and surprise. This, they say, was born of saying the word that is the birthplace of all words—Africa.

Yes, Ahh-frica.

Facing page: Reading the Good Book. From the Collections of the Library of Congress.

XAYMACA

Sailing south by east from Cuba, Columbus raised the island of Jamaica on the third of May, 1494. Still convinced that Asia lay just over the horizon, he believed that Jamaica, the Arawak-named island of "wood and water," was in fact the old continent of his impassioned inspiration. As Jamaican John Hearne writes: "He was soon to be disappointed. It was an island, like Hispaniola and Cuba, inhabited by the same Neolithic, copper-skinned, bookless innocents, whose only use for gold was ornament, not exchange." The rest we now know—or think we do. How the equable Arawak met him open-handed; how they subsequently became subjects of the Spanish crown; how their numbers decreased from close to one hundred thousand to fewer than a hundred in half that number of years.

It is a magnificent land, jungled by fairy-leaved bamboo, seven-thousand-foot mountains, dry savannahs, prickly deserts, misted valleys, silvered sands; it is a land out of an Arcadian imagination, and yet the pleasant Arawak gave it up as quickly as they deserted their bodies in the Spanish mines, and gave up their ghosts to Coyaba, their own version of heaven, which, according to the old myths, was very like the island of Jamaica. Perhaps, in leaving like a gently given breath, they knew they were only returning.

In any case, to their Spanish overlords, they were replaceable. And, in due course, the Spanish replaced them. For their faith, if such it was, was set on tangible products: spice and gold. But mainly gold. Before Columbus had even arrived in Jamaica, he

Banana Leaf. North Coast, Jamaica. Watercolor by Lisa Remeny. Tropic Arts, Coconut Grove, Florida.

had heard of it. Rumor held that the islanders collected gold from the sand, "bits the size of beans," as opposed to the poorer kind found on Hispaniola that was only "the size of grains of wheat." The island of rumor to which Columbus' heart tended to skip a beat was known as Yamaye, and so the Spanish called it Xaymaca, pronounced "ham-ay-ik-a."

At first, Columbus sent word to the Spanish sovereigns that

aboriginal Indians would make excellent slaves in Europe. However, as time went on, the myth of gold the size of beans proved as exaggerated as the Indians' "prodigious labor." Therefore, as slaves were necessary—and not, to the colonial mind, a necessary *evil*—on August 18, 1518, Ferdinand II, King of Spain, decreed that four thousand Negro slaves, both male and female, provided they be Christians, "be appropriated for useage in the Indies."

So began Jamaican slavery. Then, for two hundred years after Great Britain seized the island, the reason for its existence was not gold, but sugar. John Hearne writes:

The society created by sugar was rigid, base and greedy. It consumed life, energy and thought, and manured the industrial revolution of England with the profits from its labour. Few communities in history have ever been so unanimously dedicated to the mere production of goods at a profit; fewer yet have ever contributed less to the art, science or government of mankind. No patrician class has ever been more loutish than the Jamaican plantocracy before Emancipation; no servile class has ever had fewer examples of humane or noble principle to which they might aspire than the Jamaican slaves of the seventeenth, eighteenth and early nineteenth centuries.

During the two hundred fifty years that slavery was active in Jamaica, some thirty million Africans were brought to the New World. This was, according to the writer Stephen Davis, "the largest forced migration in human history." Among the many African people to make the journey across the Middle Passage were Ibo, Coromantee, Hausa, Mandingo, Noko, Yoruba, Sobo, and Nago nations. The miracle of survival—overcoming slavery and colonial and neocolonial subservience, all the way to the present time—is a testament of will pitted against woe. However, the insurmountable odds were met by a triumph of the human spirit. For, though the sweet land of wood and water may be severely burdened with economic ills, the people continue to rise above them. And while the collapses of Cuba and Haiti are the inheritance of unresolved neo-colonialism (Cuba's communism and Haiti's totalitarianism have at present come to the same end), there is a rainbow shining over Xaymaca. Jamaicans have an expression for how to act when things get tough: "Nah leggo." It would seem, as John Hearne has stated, that "by sheer obstinate individualism the Negro slave made possible our present society. . . . There is very little in history comparable to the scrupulous and peaceful dignity with which a nation of slaves, utterly untrained for citizenship, took up the burdens of freedom." And, we should add, are still doing so, for in the words of Jamaican poet Dennis Scott: "Only the past permits no unchaining."

YOU

Facing page: Roger Matthews and Booker T. Sapps, Bluesmen. From the Collections of the Library of Congress.

THE GOOD REVEREND, GARY DAVIS

They think that you're just a blind man; that you can't see them, ignoring you.

"You better learn how to treat everybody," you sing. Thumb pick, finger pick; hound chasing a fox on six silver strings. No one could play like that.

"Ashes to ashes and dust to dust. The life you're living won't do to trust."

They just keep ignoring you, chasing down drinks in the Fat Black Pussy Cat Café in Greenwich Village in the year of our Lord 1964. They don't know you're the last of the line; and when Old Maker laid that track, he made no more. Good old blind old black old beautiful old two-finger wizard of the six-string guitar.

"Some of you people don't realize it; taking the world by storm; don't even know how to treat your family; doing all kinds of ways; living all kinds of lives; saying everything before your children . . ."

They still don't realize the man's talking to them, us, we, the world, the gone-to-smash lowdown sorrowful place we look out at and decide to be born in before we know what we're doing.

"Ashes to ashes and dust to dust. The life you're living won't do to trust."

I stand up and thread my way through the noise and the smoke, tendrils of each tied at my ankles, wreathed round my head, and tell him: "Reverend Gary, I'm listening to you."

He says, "I'm singing for you," smiling for the first time.

—BY GERALD HAUSMAN

It was the blues, hardheaded, softhearted, and soulfully honest, that brought out a new kind of African-American music, giving birth to jazz, rock and roll, and soul. Black historian, Roger D.

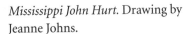
Mississippi John Hurt. Drawing by Jeanne Johns.

Abrahams has called this kind of music, in which the singer speaks to the audience and, in fact, believes his or her listeners have had the same experience, an "I-You" relationship. He cites, as an example:

Did you ever, did you ever wake up and find your baby gone?
You were so disappointed until you cried all day long.

And:

Listen folks, it's no joke
I'm as blue as I can be.

In celebrating the personal (I), the singer shares his feelings with the audience (you). You might say all music stems from this intrinsic approach, but the blues began on a different foot, so to speak, and with a different beat in mind. For one thing, it was African, at heart; it had the field holler and the shout in it; it had the lonesome whistle of a train in the night; and it had the soul, ripped up by the root and carried across the sea to God-knows-where. That's how the blues began, they say.

In the classic blues, the I-You relationship is often between two characters in the song, as if they were the only people in the world; yet the audience, the listener, is in there, as the I or the You, or both. Here is a classic Leadbelly blues titled "Pigmeat":

> *I was born in the country,*
> > *mama, but I'm staying in town*
> *If you don't believe it's pigmeat,*
> > *mama, from my head on down.*

Within the open-air saloonlike atmosphere of the blues, the singer can express his midnight, dark-down woes, as if he were the only person alive; but he is always talking, as shown above, to two central people, himself and his woman. However, in the same song comes the interlocutor, "You," who is both the "mama" of the lyric and the listening audience: "You can take me to the mountain/and there will be pigmeat there."

The technique, according to Abrahams, is the "overheard scene," the very thing that powers the blues and gives them the personal touch that was unheard before in American music. The blues—single-handedly, it seems—personalized American music with its African insistence on "audience participation." African singing and dancing are communal; so is the blues; and whether country or city, in style or tone, the You is always there, to remind us that "we" are all together in the misery, the ho-hum, business of life.

Another Africanness in the blues is the emphasis on a group

leader. Just as all African dances depend on one—as in Kumina, the spirit-dancer-leader—the blues uses a confessional person to "make us all confess our sins of loneliness and grief." The isolation of the melody and the longing of the blues are ameliorated by the You—the audience. As leader and comforter, the singer pulls all of the "You"s, the "You-all"s, into his own chant of misery or grief. "Katie May," by blues man Lightning Hopkins, is a good example:

Huddie Ledbetter and Martha Promise. From the Collections of the Library of Congress.

> *Yeah, you know Katie May's a good girl, folks*
> *And she don't run around at night*
> *Yeah, you can bet your last dollar*
> *Katie May will treat you right*
> *Yeah, you know I tried to give that woman*
> *Everything in the world she need*
> *That's why she don't do nothing*
> *But lay up in bed and read . . .*

Like other blues lyrics, this one emphasizes the personal, the particular, and the general, in that it assumes through the use of you-inclusiveness that all of us have had our share of the same. It is outright chauvinistic, except that Billie Holiday, and innumerable other blues gals, turned it back around and put the shoe on the other foot.

The blues singer, then, capitalizes on sorrow, but he or she makes it a capital affair, an inescapable human condition. As the singer takes control of the medium, the blues seeks to make us all into one; it takes the "I"s and "you"s and makes them into universal "I-owe-yous." The group leader, in the African sense of the term, is the blues singer, and he or she shares, and then manipulates us into, his way of thinking. Abrahamson states: "When his music is blue it is because his audience is rootless and unsatisfied and lonely too." He or she speaks for us all, while at the same time teaching and stroking, tenderly and roughly by turns, but always maintaining the just humility of balance. Our leader, we may say,

is falling apart, but never falling off balance. Falling, falling, but never crashing. In this dynamic relationship of the blues, anything is possible—man and woman can come together as friends, laughing and crying. And so the old teacher, the old general, the old track-layer goes right on preaching. In the words of Martin Luther King, Jr.:

> Lord, we ain't what we oughta be.
> We ain't what we wanna be.
> We ain't what we gonna be.
> But, thank God, we ain't what we was.

The blues, no matter how lowdown, is always looking up, looking out, looking on, and bringing You, whoever You are, into the simple theme of hope.

ZION

It was such a far land their voices took them to, such a far-far land. Away, away. Sun, Moon, and Stars—They Shine So Bright. It was not just the milk and honey, not just the voice of God they heard, nor even the happiness of Jesus by their sides. It was the awayness. Oh Wandering Sheep, lost and forlorn. Barren, desolate desert. Endless, arid nothingness. Day After Yesterday. Poor me, poor me. Lost and far away. Remote poor me. Dissolving me. Sweet, sweet release.
—THE CHILDREN OF SISYPHUS, *BY ORLANDO PATTERSON*

Words so familiar, so familial, like old friends, sea-washed, salt-polished pebbles on the cobbled ocean's shore. Words like Jordan, Canaan, Paradise, Zion.

What was Zion?

Zion was, for the African-American slave, a dream, a rhythm, a way of life where there was no suffering; a song, a deliverance, a banner, a rebellion, and a geographical place. In the dream Zion, there was an angel with a mark on his forehead and a harp in his hand. Segregated, yes; slave, no. There was, as we can see, a tinge of realism in the Zion of dreams. The other Zion, the physical one, was in Liberia, or Ethiopia, or anywhere in Africa. For Africa itself was Zion. There could be no other. In this Zion, the bells did not toll for thee to leave, but to stay. A man, a woman might walk as much as he or she pleased, and sit down at will. And a spiritual fortune might result in such idleness. This Zion, of course, was no less a dream in physical form than the other one was in the psyche. In reality, the passage to Zion was costly in all possible ways.

The transportation of Negroes to Zion was, however, more hazardous than anyone anticipated. When the Harriet sailed to Liberia in 1829, the casualties among the emigrants were checked in red ink. There were 18 Negroes who were reported as having died on that vessel and 23 on the Liberia. No less than 56 out of 106 emigrants who started to Africa on the Montgomery in 1830 succumbed. That year colonizationists stopped recording the deaths of emigrants. Of the 382 Negroes who sailed to Africa that year, 143 of them died, over 37 per cent.

The name, age, occupation, residence in the United States, and time of emigration were recorded for each emigrant. A record was also kept giving the ship upon which each emigrant sailed. Negroes registered in advance for sailings to Africa and by about 1832 asked questions, in song, about the ships upon which they were to embark. Questions like: "Where from?" "How laden?" "Who is the captain?" etc. About ten years later Negroes of Anne Arundel County, Maryland, sang:

Facing page: Boo, the Carver (at Work on Black Angel). Port Maria, Jamaica. Photograph by Leah.

What ship is that [be] you're enlisted upon?
O glory hallelujah!

(Chorus:)
'Tis the old ship of Zion, hallelujah!
'Tis the old ship of Zion, hallelujah!
—FROM AMERICAN NEGRO SLAVE SONGS BY MILES MARK FISHER.

Set against Zion, in diametric opposition, was Satan. In the era that followed the insurrection of Nat Turner, many African Americans believed that their civil rights would always be denied. The legend that supported this fear held that Satan himself said that blacks could never be free in America. The following spiritual was preserved on Port Royal Island, but its place of origin was perhaps Southampton County, Virginia:

Old Satan told [tell] me to my face,
O yes, Lord,
De God I seek I never find,
O yes, Lord.
True believer, I know when I gwine home,
True believer, I know when I gwine home,
True believer, I know when I gwine home,
I been afraid to die.

Sometimes it works the other way around, but usually mythology is supported by history. It is interesting to note that, at the time of the Nat Turner Rebellion, Virginia blacks were actually being put into jail at Jerusalem, Virginia. Add to this, the patrol call of the cavalry trumpet, the zeal of missionaries planting biblical seeds night and day, and it is not hard to understand how African Americans might dream of being expatriated to Liberia, West Africa. Liberia was to slaves what Ethiopia has become for Rastafarians, a "new Jerusalem."

There is no doubt in the minds of Rastafarians that Ethiopia is the Zion spoken of in the Bible. The site of King David's throne, it is mentioned in the second chapter of Genesis, verse 13: "And the name of the second river is Gi-hon: the same is it that compasseth the whole land of Ethiopia." To further galvanize the myth, Psalm 68, verse 4, celebrates the name of Jah: "Sing unto God, sing praises to his name: extol him that rideth upon the heavens by his name JÄH, and rejoice before him." And perhaps the most quoted of all biblical passages in the Rasta brotherhood, verse 31 of the same psalm: "Princes shall come out of Egypt; Ethiopia shall soon stretch out her hands unto God."

In his book *Dread,* Joseph Owen makes the clear statement that Zion does not refer to Jerusalem in Palestine:

The Rastafarians simply say that the gospels clearly demonstrate that Jesus forsook that Jerusalem and the whole land of Palestine, and called his people to a new Jerusalem, which is Ethiopia. The prolonged and futile war now going on in the Middle East is a clear manifestation of the folly of the "so-called" Jews in trying to re-establish the old Zion.

Clearly, apart from all religious inquiry, Zion, unclothed, is a synonym for an otherworld where the perfect life is lived. It is the Garden of Eden prior to the Fall; Atlantis prior to sinking into the sea; and all other Utopias and Erewhons combined—no poverty, only plenty; grapes within reach, water in abundance, and neither heat, nor cold, nor pestilence. Zion, where work, as such, is unknown and love is the law, where civil rights consist of mere being and mere breathing, where man is exalted and woman is praised, and where, as the slave said who sat down in Zion, "A fortune might result from such idleness."

Black Angel by Boo. Photograph by Bobbe Besold.

GLOSSARY OF MYTHS

ANANCY: Also spelled *Anansi*, the spidergod of Africa, was once a man whose present incarnation is man/spider, like Spiderman, the comic strip hero; however, he is part of the long lineage of African tricksters, those who do well and ill, by turns. In the West Indies, he surfaces as a figure called Uncle Time, a cross between Father Time and a playful uncle.

ANCESTOR: The bond that exists between Africa and the New World was, for many African Americans, kept alive through the old system of ancestor worship inherent in many African religions, where death is merely another stage of life.

BUFFALO SOLDIER: The American Indians, particularly the Cheyenne, saw in the black calvary units that protected the Frontier, a mythical resemblance to the buffalo. Buffalo Soldier was a term of warrior-respect because the black men fought so well; physically, the term depicted the curly hair of the men themselves.

DOG: To many African tribes the dog was a deity because he was a friend of God and one of the first beings of creation. As fire-bringer and animal pursuer, Dog proved invaluable to the first hunters. In the New World, Dog turns up as a deified, if comic, sidekick for humanity, but it was his ancient African use as a guardian of women that is celebrated in the West Indies today.

DRUM: The hollow log drum is associated with speech and communication. The skin drum adds yet another aspect to the relationship between man and god, man and man; it is an inter-

locutor, a medium for spirit talk. When drumming was outlawed on the plantations because of the rebellious influence
that the colonials believed it inspired, the slaves turned to
another drumlike instrument, the banjo, with which they bur-
lesqued their white rulers in song and dance.

COTTON TREE: Trees of many kinds are spiritual to Africans, who
regard their soaring height, reaching into the skies, as a
metaphorical way of joining heaven and earth. The souls of the
dead are also thought to inhabit certain trees, especially the
larger ones such as the West Indian cotton and the guango tree,
both of which originated on African soil.

DUPPY: Also called jumbie in certain parts of the West Indies, this
supernatural character is a ghost. By means of obeah and vaudou, such spirits were often called into action and used for
their supernatural advantage against the living, particularly the
cruel masters of plantations.

ELEPHANT: The presence of the elephant in African mythology
often symbolizes kindness and sorrow, as if its great size also
encompassed all the tribulations of life. As the text states, "He is
stone; he is grief; he is love unrequited."

FATHER: Synonymous with God's love, the myth of the father is
one of mystical union with woman and child. In African-
American and West Indian communities where ideal fatherhood is revered, the notion of father is threefold: Father (God);
Father (husband); Father (Africa).

GLORY: In mythological terms this can be expressed as heaven or
paradise, as well as exaltation and religious ecstasy. Glory is
both noun and adjective, place and feeling.

GOURD: The famous song "Follow the Drinking Gourd" referred
to the shape of the Big Dipper and how it pointed North. During slave times, the star gourd led the way North to freedom.
Basically, the gourd, or gourdy, was used as a dipper of water.
However, its other uses (such as using the pulp to draw out
poison) lend mythical credence to its power on earth as well as
the sky.

HAND: A potent metaphor for healing and holiness, as in "the laying on of hands." Originally, in African myth, hands symbolized a man's power—"the brush of a hand." In contemporary times, the hand motif is largely expressed in music, particularly by the players of stringed instruments, singers, and dancers.

HEART: African Americans and West Indians often refer to the heart as if it were a person rather than the primary metaphor for feeling, as it is commonly used in European mythology. The concept of the heart-person goes back to ancient Egypt and Africa.

JONKONNU: (Also John Canoe) A combination of Creole mythology (animal and human costumes), Jonkonnu is a form of West African sorcery, which entered the New World as a kind of folk dance that turned masquerade and poked satiric fun at European plantation masters and mistresses. At Christmas time in the Caribbean, one can see Jonkonnu dancers whose spirit is, today, one of pure revelry. However, the dancers also like to remind children that "they'd better be good," in much the same way that Hopi Kachina dancers warn their children.

LION: Although the myths of lions in Africa are varied, the deeper impression that has been cast over the centuries is a comparison between the lion and kingliness. The princely line of Judah, stemming from the time of King Solomon, was, and is, a lineage of lions. Today's Rastas have embodied the lion myth into their concept of manliness, fatherhood, and proximity to Haile Selassie, a true lion king of Ethiopia. The image of the lion as ruler and symbol of power extends far back in time and includes the Pharaohs of ancient Egypt and the contemporary Kikuyu and Masai people.

MERMAID: Tales of fish women emanate from Africa and Europe and have become entwined with Amerindian myths. Eighteenth- and nineteenth-century mariners from the British Isles spun stories about legendary sirens, fabled sulkies (seal people), and other water-mother myths they heard told by American Indians. The African-American people mixed all of these together into a kind of gumbo of tale telling; the fish woman, therefore, is good and bad, comic and tragic, and embodies end-of-quest treasure from the three cultures that have given birth to her.

MOTHER: The concept of Mother Africa is the subject of songs, poems, and multiple myths. As Earth Mother of the world, Mama Africa, as she has come to be known, is representative of the virtues of protection, care-giving, familial blessing, and bounty from the earth's cornucopia. While Father as a mythological symbol may have some aspects lacking in tenderness (as in Native American mythology of Sun Father, who is, at times, very stern and admonishing), Mama Africa (as in Native American mythology of Mother Earth, who is ultimately responsible for all living beings) is always the nurturing female presence, whose sole purpose is protection of her offspring.

NINE NIGHT: A West Indian practice similar to an Irish Wake wherein the spirit of the dead is given nine nights of special attendance before being sent on its way into the afterworld. This old custom, stemming from African ancestor religion, relies on a good and proper send-off to the spirit world, so that the spirit will not seek revenge, or be uneasy, on its journey.

PARADISE: The world of the spirit seems to exist in most African myths as a land above this one, although there are some that contradict this, notably certain myths that depict a world similar to ours just underneath the surface of the earth. However, as in Elizabethan cosmology, the world above this one is thought to be ideal because of its proximity to God. Often a grand tree or a great mountain is the stairway to heaven, the ladder to the Lord. Although there is no guarantee to perfection in "paradise," African myths celebrate it as a place of power. African Americans have made this myth over, as have West Indians, turning paradise into the "here and now." In this way, it may be related to the term Glory, and can be entered by the mediums of music and dance, and, in the case of Rastas, the ceremonial and meditative use of the ganga plant.

RIVER: In Africa, water myths come replete with water gods and goddesses. Water is a medium of purification, a divine cleanser of flesh and spirit. In America these concepts became enmeshed in biblical imagery of river crossings and baptisms and watery rites of passage. The power of water as a purifier was, and is, equally potent to Amerindian and Native American people.

ROCK: The first art ever inscribed by man was on rock, so it is fitting that the oral metaphor of the rock should be a symbol for man and earth combined. Mainly, in myths, the rock bears witness, but it cannot hide the miscreant or sinner in the Bible. The rock is also the testament to flesh: Eventually, no matter how strong, it withers away, leaving only swirling sand, or spirit. In slave times, due to the influence of the Bible, the rock became a symbol for the church, the place of rest, the sanctuary from the flood.

SERPENT: While in the Christian biblical sense, the serpent represents unwanted knowledge and the fall from grace, in African culture, the snake is a powerful god. In vaudou, it is Damballah, the tail swallower, comparable to Quetzacoatl, the Feathered Serpent of Indian America. The serpent is used today in religious ceremonies in Haiti and by the descendants of white European settlers in the mountains of Appalachia. In Jamaica, the snake is generally feared, while in Haiti (a close distance away), it is generally loved and/or respected. Both attitudes are tribally oriented, but one must consider the pervasive influence of the Bible on the old African earth religions and the reaction of missionaries, priests, and preachers, who were appalled by African people using snakes in ceremonies.

SIGN: African-American signs of the nineteenth century covered everything from numbers to water falling from the sky and from cotton blowing on the wind to roosters crowing and lizards shedding their tails. All things were traceable to symptom and sign. Unexplained events were always of a certain mysterious inclination that could be good or bad. Such potent signs were interpreted in Africa by shamans, but in the Americas these became known as hoodoo men, obeah men and women, myal men and women, shepherds (usually women), mothers, captains, kumina priests, root and bush doctors, papalois and hougans, and other workers of mystery and magic.

TRICKSTER: The nature of the divine trickster in West Africa is bound with the concept of Fate. Africans have a great belief in Fate, but it is not irrevocable; it can be bargained, bartered, or otherwise tampered with. Enter the Trickster. This personage, often cast as a child, is the intermediary to the gods. Given such power he or she might put in a bid of favor for some mortal, just as the Greek interlocutors were often apt to do. Yet, just the same, since tricksters are capricious, things could go the other way around, as well. It depends, of course, on the trickster in question and the deity whose favor is sought. The legend told by Uncle Remus, the folkloric creation of Joel Chandler Harris, whose Brer Rabbit became the most famous trickster of the Deep South, was of a rabbit too tricky for Brer Fox and others to catch. The lessons learned by youngsters reading Harris in the nineteenth century were similar to Aesop's Fables, moral tales of thinly screened allegory with sketchy animal lore as embroidery. The origin of these stories has always been questionable, but it is fairly safe to assume that most of them are a mixture of Cherokee and/or Creek myths smoothly rendered into African-sounding tales, which, nonetheless, have plenty of the West African trickster lore in them. Part African, part Creek? No one really knows how much is borrowed from either culture, and, adding to the confusion is the fact that the stories also have plenty of parallels in European mythology. Ultimately, though, it must be admitted that Harris, regardless of his sources, was a good enough storyteller for the fables to stick around for well over one hundred years.

VAUDOU: According to Herbert Gold in his fine book on Haiti, *The Best Nightmare on Earth:* "A mixture of Christian and African beliefs, voodoo is a religion with rich ceremonies, rituals, observances, and consolations. It offers a view of the world and a hope for the future. And alongside voodoo there is also the parallel world of white magic and black magic, the system of curses and devils." Eugene Aubin, a French writer who lived in Haiti prior to 1898, stated: "From the medley of purely African voodoo tradition brought over by the slaves from all parts of Africa, two principal rites became predominant, the Guinea rite and the Congo rite. The Guinea rite is predominant in the matter of beliefs and superstitions—the Congo, perhaps in practice." Zora Neale Hurston's vaudou studies are classic, for she was the first prominent African-American writer and anthropologist to delve into the subject, not by making assumptions, but by experiencing the rituals themselves, interviewing vaudou priests, and then, when she had meditated fully on the meaning of what she'd seen, wrote about it in clear, poetical prose, which, to this day (sixty years later), no one has bettered.

WATER: As stated in the book, "Ancient Egyptians believed that water was a sacred purifier, not only in a superficial sense but in the transmission of divine grace." Water, particularly in Southern Baptist practice, confers beatitude and solemnity, which is why the baptismal rites were so readily adopted by African-Americans, whose own heritage combined so many water purification ceremonies. As a medium for passage, as across the ocean, water also appears in myths of repatriation and return to Africa.

WORD: In African earth religion, the power of the word was heard in nature, as in the singing grass, the threshing grain, the thrumming drum. Since the literature of Africa began, as all literature does, on the tongue, the myths are spoken with a certain measure and cadence that is uniquely African; and yet one hears in these stories the same voice that informs the wisdom literature of Native America. The word, born of breath and the moisture of the mouth, is life. And life is sacred. Therefore, no amount of words can convey the power of the deeply drawn, the softly exhaled breath. The intent of storytelling, African style, is to do honor to the life-force contained in human speech, and to give the release of birth to each word so that it goes up to the creator, who bears witness to all things.

ZION: The concept of Zion for African-Americans shifted ever so slightly from a biblical place of rest to the homeland, Africa. As a symbol or repatriation, Zion became the dreaming man and woman's answered prayer of return to integrity, to Africa, to a land, as Mutabaruka states, "where man act like man." Today, the idea of Zion is the bright place of promise for Rastas whose faith decrees that the world of disharmony that we live in, at large, is Babylon and the only true place of dignity for man is Zion. These terms are metaphysical, but there is, as well, a hue of geography attached to them. Just as slaves dreamed of being set free and traveling home to Liberia, Rastafarians speak of Ethiopia as their true home and the foundation of their faith in Africa. Thus is Zion a spiritual and physical place, a geography of the journeying soul.

NOTES

AMISTAD: Research by Terri Lynne Singleton; "The *Amistad* Event," The United Church Board for Homeland Ministries, 1994.

ANCESTOR: Research by Kelvin Rodriques; "The New Ships" Edward Brathwaite in *New Ships*, edited by D. G. Wilson; interview with Richard Tito Ama recorded in Kenya by Ross LewAllen in 1987; the Heptones' lyric from "The Book of Rules," as quoted in *Reggae Bloodlines*, Stephen Davis and Peter Simon; "Brothers and Sisters," Ziggy Marley, from *Joy and Blues*, Ziggy Marley and the Melody Makers.

BANJO: *The Negro and His Folklore*, edited by Bruce Jackson; *The Art and Times of the Guitar*, Frederic V. Grunfeld.

BUFFALO SOLDIER: Jet, April 11, 1994.

CHURCH: *The Children of Sisyphus*, Orlando Patterson.

CONJURE: "Stagolee," Sid Hausman; interview with Jenny Smith by Gerald Hausman at Castle Gordon, Jamaica, West Indies, 1993; *The Magic Island*, William Seabrook; *Fabulous New Orleans*, Lyle Saxon.

DRUM: "The Making of the Drum," Edward Brathwaite, *New Ships*, edited by D. G. Wilson; "The Shona Drum Legend" from "The Ngoma and Muridzi we Ngoma of the Shona Peoples," recorded in Zimbabwe by Seth Cohen in 1991.

ELEPHANT: "Elephants" Burning Spear (Winston Rodney) from *Jah Kingdom*, Burning Music Productions; "Poem for Elephants," Ross LewAllen.

FATHER: Interview with Mackie McDonnough, Roy McKay, and
   Benji Oswald Brown by Gerald Hausman, Blue Harbour,
   Jamaica, West Indies, 1986–1988.
GLORY: "In Africa," from *Walk About My World*, Ross LewAllen;
   Tell My Horse, Zora Neale Hurston; "The Glory Trumpeter,"
   Derek Walcott, from *Collected Poems: 1948–1984*.
GOURD: Traditional American folk song, "Follow the Drinking
   Gourd"; research by Mariah Fox Hausman; Publications of the
   Texas Folklore Society, Volume 7, 1928, pp 81–84, reprinted
   from *Mother Wit from the Laughing Barrel*, edited by Alan
   Dundes.
HAND: Research by Terri Lynne Singleton; *The Hand of Destiny:
   Folklore and Superstition for Everyday Life*, C. J. S. Thompson.
HEART: Research by Terri Lynne Singleton; *African Folktales*,
   edited by Charlotte and Wolf Leslau.
INDIGO: Research by Terri Lynne Singleton; poem by Terri
   Lynne Singleton; *Stitched from the Soul: Slave Quilts from the
   Antebellum South*, Gladys-Marie Fry; *Into Indigo: African Tex-
   tiles and Dyeing Techniques*, Claire Polakoff; *The American
   Quilt: A History of Cloth and Comfort 1750–1950*, Mary Eliza-
   beth Johnson.
JIVE: Research by David Dalby, reader in West African Languages,
   British School of Oriental and African Studies, London; *The
   Subterraneans*, Jack Kerouac.
JUBA: *Step It Down: Games, Plays, Songs and Stories from the
   Afro-American Heritage*, Bessie Jones and Bess Lomax Hanes.
KEBRA NEGAST: *The Queen of Sheba and Her only Son
   Menyelek*, (author(s) unknown); Interview with Sheldon
   Campbell, Liguanea, Jamaica, 1993.
KUMINA: *A-Z of Jamaican Heritage*, Olive Senior.
LION: *African Folktales*, edited by Paul Radin; *Longing for Dark-
   ness*, Peter Beard; "The Lion Leaps," Ross LewAllen, from an
   unpublished African journal.
MERMAID: *American Negro Folktales*, Richard M. Dorson;
   African Folktales, edited by Charlotte and Wolf Leslau; *Duppy

Talk: West Indian Tales of Mystery and Magic, Gerald Hausman; *The Sun Horse: Native Visions of the New World,* Gerald Hausman.

MOTHER: Research by Terri Lynne Singleton. *Double Stitch: Black Women Write about Mothers and Daughters,* edited by Patricia Bell-Scott; *African Folktales,* edited by Charlotte and Wolf Leslau.

NAME: "Names of American Negro Slaves" by Newbell Niles Puckett, from *Mother Wit from the Laughing Barrel,* Alan Dundes.

OBEAH: "I Know a Man, Wicked of Ways," Gerald Hausman, from *Duppies, Drum Talk & Obeah Men: West Indian and Caribbean Folktales Duppy Talk: West Indian Tales of Mystery and Magic,* Gerald Hausman.

PARADISE: Research by Mariah Fox Hausman; *Lilies of the Field,* William E. Barrett; *Mythology of All Races,* edited by Alice Werner.

QUILT: Research and text by Terri Lynne Singleton; *Double Stitch: Black Women Write about Mothers and Daughters,* Patricia Bell-Scott; *Stitched from the Soul: Slave Quilts from the Antebellum South,* Gladys-Marie Fry; "Kuba Embroidered Cloth," Monni Adams, *African Arts,* Volume 12, 1978.

RAP: *The Negro and His Folklore,* edited by Bruce Jackson; "Hip-Hop Goes to the Head of the Class," Jody Mailander, *The Miami Herald,* June 12, 1994.

RIVER: "Ballad of My Two Grandfathers," Nicolas Guillen, trans. G. R. Coulthard, from *New Ships,* edited by D. G. Wilson; *The Everglades: River of Grass,* Marjory Stoneman Douglas; *The Adventures of Huckleberry Finn,* Mark Twain; "Rivers of Love," Gerald Hausman, from *Duppies, Drum Talk & Obeah Men: West Indian and Caribbean Folktales; Deep Like the Rivers,* Martha Emmons.

SERPENT: "Saving Haiti's Soul," John Donnelly, *The Miami Herald,* June 12, 1994; *Mama Lola: A Vodou Priestess in Brooklyn,* Karen McCarthy Brown.

SIGN: *A Treasury of American Folklore*, edited by B. A. Botkin; *Tell My Horse*, Zora Neale Hurston; "Symptom and Sign," from *Heart Feel It* by Foundation; research by Kelvin Rodriques.

SOUL: Interview with Mackie McDonnough by Gerald Hausman, Blue Harbour, Jamaica, West Indies, 1986–1988; *African Folktales*, edited by Charlotte and Wolf Leslau; research by Kelvin Rodriques.

TRACK: *A Treasury of Railroad Folklore*, edited by B. A. Botkin and Alvin F. Harlow.

TRICKSTER: *Witchcraft, Mysticism and Magic in the Black World*, James Haskins.

TURTLE: Research by Alicia Lauritzen; interview with Rupert DaCosta by Gerald Hausman, Blue Harbour, Jamaica, West Indies, 1993.

TRINITY: Research by Kelvin Rodriques; interview with Janice Kallou by Gerald Hausman, Bokeelia and Miami, Florida, May, 1995.

UNCLE TIME: *Duppy Talk: West Indian Tales of Mystery and Magic*, Gerald Hausman; interview with Benji Oswald Brown by Gerald Hausman, Blue Harbour, Jamaica, West Indies, 1987.

UNDERGROUND RAILROAD: "Underground Railroad," by Charles L. Blockson, pp 3–39, *National Geographic*, July, 1984.

VAUDON: *Witchcraft, Mysticism and Magic in the Black World*, James Haskins.

WATER: *Mother Wit from the Laughing Barrel*, Alan Dundes.

WEST: "The Forgotten Pioneers," Scott Minerbrook, pp 53–55, *U.S. News & World Report*, August 8, 1994.

WORD: *Zora Is My Name*, produced by Pacific Arts Video, 1990; "Faith, Love, Peace and God," Kelvin Rodriques.

XAYMACA: *Ian Fleming Introduces Jamaica*, Morris Cargill.

YOU: *Positively Black*, Roger Abrahams; "The Good Reverend Gary Davis," Gerald Hausman; interview with Reverend Gary Davis by Gerald and Sid Hausman, The Fat Black Pussy Cat, Greenwich Village, NY, 1964.

ZION: *Negro Slave Songs in the United States*, Miles Mark Fisher.

BIBLIOGRAPHY

Abrahams, Roger. *Positively Black.* Englewood, N.J.: Prentice-Hall, 1970.

Adams, Emilie. *Understanding Jamaican Patois: An Introduction to Afro-Jamaican Grammar.* Kingston, Jamaica: Kingston Publishers, 1992.

"Amistad Event", Cleveland: The United Church Board for Homeland Ministries, 1984.

Beard, Peter. *Longing for Darkness.* New York: Harcourt Brace, 1975.

Bell-Scott, Patricia. *Double Stitch: Black Women Write about Mothers and Daughters.* Boston, Beacon Press, 1991.

Berry, James. *Celebration Song.* New York: Willa Perlman Books/Harper Collins, 1991.

Berry, James. *Ajeemah and His Son.* New York: Willa Perlman Books/Harper Collins, 1991.

Bollingham Foundation. *African Folktales and Sculpture.* New York: Pantheon, 1952.

Botkin, B. A. *A Treasury of Southern Folklore.* New York: Crown, 1949.

Botkin B. A. and Harlow, A. *A Treasury of Railroad Folklore.* New York: Bonanza Books, 1953.

Brawley, Benjamin. *Early Black American Writers.* Toronto: Dover Publishers, 1992.

Brooks, Lester. *Great Civilizations of Ancient Africa.* New York: Four Winds, 1971.

Brown, Karen McCarthy. *Mama Lola: A Vodou Priestess in Brook-lyn.* Berkeley: University of California Press, 1992.

"Buffalo Soldier." *Jet,* April 11, 1994. p. 32.

"Buli Master and Other Hands, The," *Art in America*, Vol. 68(5): 980. pp. 132–142.

Cargill, Morris. *Ian Fleming Introduces Jamaica.* London: Andre Deutsch, 1965.

Cassidy, Frederic. *Jamaica Talk: Three Hundred Years of the English Language in Jamaica.* London: Macmillan Caribbean, 1982.

Cornish, Sam. *Generations.* Boston: Beacon Press, 1971.

Cornish, Sam. *Grandmother's Pictures.* Lenox, Mass.: The Book-store Press, 1974.

Davis, Stephen and Simon, Peter. *Reggae Bloodlines: In Search of the Music and Culture of Jamaica.* New York: Anchor, 1979.

Dorson, Richard M. *American Negro Folktales.* Greenwich, Conn.: Fawcett , 1967.

Douglas, Marjory Stoneman. *The Everglades: River of Grass.* Mari-etta, Georgia: Mockingbird Books, 1974.

Dundes, Alan. *Mother Wit from the Laughing Barrel.* Garland, 1981.

Drimmer, Melvin. *Black History: A Reappraisal.* Garden City, New York: Doubleday, 1968.

Emmons, Martha. *Deep Like the Rivers: Stories of my Negro Friends.* Nacogdoches, Texas: Texas Folklore Society, 1969.

Felton, Humphrey. *Jamaica Journal.* Kingston, Jamaica: Institute of Jamaica Archive, 1890.

Fisher, Miles Mark. *Negro Slave Songs in the United States.* Ithaca, New York: Cornell University Press, 1953.

"Forgotten Pioneers, The," *U.S. News & World Report.* Scott Minerbrook. August 8, 1994, pp. 53–55.

Fry, Gladys-Marie. *Stitched from the Soul: Slave Quilts from the Antebellum South.* Athens, Georgia: University of Georgia Press, 1993.

Gold, Herbert. *Best Nightmare on Earth: A Life in Haiti.* New York: Prentice Hall, 1991.

Grunfeld, Frederic. *The Art and Times of the Guitar.* London: Macmillan, 1969.

Haskins, James. *Witchcraft, Mysticism and Magic in the Black World.* New York: Doubleday, 1974.

Hatch, John. *Africa Today and Tomorrow.* New York: Praeger Inc., 1965.

Hausman, Gerald. *Duppy Talk: West Indian Tales of Mystery and Magic.* New York: Simon and Schuster Inc., 1994.

Hausman, Gerald. *The Sun Horse.* Silver Lake, Wis.: Lotus Light, 1993.

Hemingway, Ernest. *Islands in the Stream.* New York: Scribners, 1970.

Hersey, John. *Key West Tales.* New York: Knopf, 1993.

"Hip-Hop Goes to the Head of the Class." Jody Mailander, *The Miami Herald,* June 12, 1994.

The Holy Bible.: King James Version

Hotchkiss, Bill. *The Medicine Calf.* New York: W. W. Norton, 1981.

Hudson, Mark. *Our Grandmother's Drums.* New York: Grove Weidenfeld, 1989.

Hurston, Zora Neale. *Dust Tracks on a Road.* New York: Harper Collins, 1991.

Hurston, Zora Neale. *Tell My Horse.* New York: HarperCollins, 1990.

Huxley, Elspeth. *Nine Faces of Kenya.* New York: Penguin, 1990.

Insight Guide to Jamaica. Englewood, New Jersey: Prentice Hall, 1984.

Jackson, Bruce. *The Negro and His Folklore.* Austin, Texas: University of Texas Press, 1967.

Johnson, Mary Elizabeth. *The American Quilt: A History of Cloth and Comfort 1750–1950.* New York: Potter, 1993.

Kebra Negast, The Queen of Sheba and Her Only Son Menyelek. London: The Medici Society, 1922.

Kerouac, Jack. *The Subterraneans.* New York: Avon, 1958.

Kincaid, Jamaica. *At The Bottom of the River.* New York: Vintage, 1985.

Larousse Encyclopedia of Mythology. New York: Prometheus Press, 1959.

Leslau, Charlotte and Wolf. *African Folktales.* Brattleboro, Vt.: The Peter Pauper Press, 1963.

LewAllen, Ross. *Walk About My World.* Unpublished Journal, 1990.

Lyons, Mary. *Sorrow's Kitchen: The Life and Folklore of Zora Neale Hurston.* New York: Scribners, 1990.

Naylor, Gloria. *Mama Day.* New York: Vintage, 1989.

Naipaul, V.S. *A Way In The World.* New York: Knopf, 1994.

Owens, Joseph. *Dread: The Rastafarian in Jamaica.* Kingston, Jamaica: Sangster, 1976.

Patterson, Orlando. *The Children of Sisyphus.* London, Longman, 1964.

Phillips, Caryl. *Cambridge.* New York: Knopf, 1992.

Polakoff, Claire. *Into Indigo: African Textiles and Dyeing Techniques.* New York: Doubleday, 1980.

Ranchard, Kenneth and Gray, Cecil. *West Indian Poetry: An Anthology for Schools.* Trinidad & Jamaica: Longman, 1971.

Robertson, Diane. *Jamaican Herbs: Nutritional and Medicinal Values.* Kingston, Jamaica: Jamaican Herbs Ltd., 1986.

Sachs, Wulf. *Black Hamlet.* Boston: Little Brown & Co., 1947.

Sackheim, Eric and Shahn, Jonathan. *The Blues Line.* New York:Grossman Publishers, 1969.

Salkey, Andrew. *Island Voices* New York: Liveright, 1970.

Saxon, Lyle and Tallant. *Gumbo Ya Ya.* Boston: Houghton Mifflin, 1945.

Saxon, Lyle. *Fabulous New Orleans.* New York: The Century Co., 1928.

Schwarz-Bart, Andre. *A Woman Named Solitude.* New York: Atheneum, 1973.

Seabrook, William. *The Magic Island.* New York: Paragon House, 1989.

Senior, Olive. *A-Z of Jamaican Heritage.* Kingston, Jamaica: The Gleaner Co., 1988.

Senior, Olive. *Summer Lightning.* Trinidad: Longman Caribbean, 1986.

Shoumatoff, Alex. *Florida Ramble.* New York: Vintage Books, 1974.

Thompson, C. J. S. *The Hand of Destiny: Folklore and Superstition for Everyday Life.* New York: Bell Publishing, 1989.

Tutuola, Amos. *My Life in the Bush of Ghosts.* London: Faber and Faber, 1954.

Tutuola, Amos. *The Palm-Wine Drinkard.* New York: Grove Press, 1953.

Twain, Mark. *The Adventures of Huckleberry Finn.* New York: Signet Classic, 1959.

"Underground Railroad," *The National Geographic.* Charles L. Blockson. July, 1984, Volume 166, No. 1, pp. 3–39.

Walcott, Derek. *The Antilles.* New York: Farrar, Strauss & Giroux, 1992.

Walcott, Derek. *Collected Poems: 1948–1984.* New York: Farrar, Strauss & Giroux, 1986.

Wallace, David Rains. *Bulow Hammock: Mind in a Forest.* San Francisco: Sierra Club Books, 1988.

Werner, Alice. *The Mythology of All Races.* African Vol. 7. New York: Cooper Square Publishers, 1964.

White, Timothy. *Catch a Fire: The Life of Bob Marley.* New York: Henry Holt, 1989.

Williams, Joy. *The Florida Keys.* New York: Random House, 1991.

Wilentz, Amy. *The Rainy Season.* New York: Touchstone Books, 1990.

Williams, Eric. *Documents of West Indian History,* Trinidad: PNM Publishing Co., 1963.

Wilson, Donald G. *New Ships: An Anthology of West Indian Poetry for Secondary Schools.* London: Oxford University Press, 1975.

ABOUT THE AUTHORS

GERALD HAUSMAN has been a professional storyteller as well as a writer, editor, and mythologist. His special areas of dedication are Native America, the Caribbean, and Central Europe, and his many published books testify to his love of these cultures and places. In 1985, Mr. Hausman and his wife, Lorry, founded the Blue Harbour School of Creative Writing in Port Maria, Jamaica, West Indies.

This institution (housed on the grounds of Noël Coward's old estate) brought together American, Native American, West Indian, and Hispanic students of various ages and points of view and gave them and opportunity to share culturally while getting to know the island of Jamaica. It was during the past ten years, while teaching in Jamaica, that Mr. Hausman and his wife saw an educational need for a book that would combine the spirit and root cultures of Africa, Amerindia, and the West Indies, showing their connection to black American life today. Working with Kelvin Rodriques brought this ideal into a clearly focused goal.

Mr. Hausman credits his interest in West African culture to many influences: "I have been lucky over the past twenty or so years to have worked with some truly great teachers of the mystic arts, including Kelvin Rodriques. Running the school in Jamaica has been one of the hardest and most blessed experiences of all, proving, through financial adversity, bad weather and drought, too many students, and not enough food, that, as Bob Marley said, 'When one door closes, another opens.'"

KELVIN RODRIQUES, a teacher of martial arts and mathematics, is a well-known Southwestern broadcaster whose program, *The Iyah Music Show*, is very popular among American Indian, African-American, and other listeners of all ages. Mr. Rodriques was born and raised in Tunapuna, Trinidad, after which he moved to New York City and later, to Sante Fe. There, after completing his degree in business at the College of Sante Fe, he began to write, to teach, and to reach listeners through the art of story-telling and Caribbean music on KUNM radio. He has also produced reggae music programs, most recently Burning Spear at Paoli Soleri, Sante Fe.

Mr. Rodriques's gift as a spontaneous speaker originates, as he puts it, when "someone is willing to listen to me, and something inside me resonates with them. The magical things in this book become real to me when I share them with someone else: Cool evenings under bright moons brought back my childhood in Trinidad. These were the cultural events that shaped, and still affect, my life. This book is timely because we are living in an age when many others are seeking how to be more loving, more spiritual, more connected with others. The stories and revelations herein will help them to do so."